विवेकशतकम्
Viveka-śatakam
A Hundred Verses of Wisdom

श्रीचैतन्यचित्राष्टकम्
Śrī Caitanya-citrāṣṭakam

and

श्रीनित्यानन्दाष्टकम्
Śrī Nityānandāṣṭakam

Other Publications from Bhakti Vikas Trust

Books by His Holiness Bhakti Vikāsa Swami

A Beginner's Guide to Kṛṣṇa Consciousness
A Message to the Youth of India
Brahmacarya in Kṛṣṇa Consciousness
Glimpses of Traditional Indian Life
Jaya Śrīla Prabhupāda!
Lekha-mālā
Mothers and Masters
My Memories of Śrīla Prabhupāda
On Pilgrimage in Holy India
On Speaking Strongly in Śrīla Prabhupāda's Service
Patropadeśa (two volumes)
Rāmāyaṇa
Śrī Bhaktisiddhānta Vaibhava (three volumes)
Śrī Caitanya Mahāprabhu
Śrī Vaṁśīdāsa Bābājī
The Story of Rasikānanda
Gauḍīya Vaiṣṇava Padyāvalī (Bengali)
Vaiṣṇava Śikhā o Sādhana (Bengali)

Books by Other Authors

Śrī Cāṇakya-nīti (by Patita Pāvana Dāsa Adhikārī)
Rethinking Darwin (by Lalitānātha Dāsa)
Who is Supreme? (by Gokula Candra Dāsa)

|| *Śrī-Śrī-Gaurāṅga-Nityānandau jayataḥ* ||

श्रीप्रबोधानन्दसरस्वतीप्रणीतं

विवेकशतकम्

Viveka-śatakam

A Hundred Verses of Wisdom

श्रीचैतन्यचित्राष्टकम्

Śrī Caitanya-citrāṣṭakam

and

श्रीनित्यानन्दाष्टकम्

Śrī Nityānandāṣṭakam

by

Prabodhānanda Sarasvatī

Critically edited and translated from the original in Sanskrit

by Demian Martins (PhD)

Bhakti Vikas Trust

Cover picture: *"Kṛṣṇa speaks with the animals of Vṛndāvana,"* by Puskar dasa (© Matthew Goldman), puskarpaintings.com

Cover design by Bhismadeva dasa, HoofprintMedia.com

ISBN: 978-93-82109-42-6

www.bvks.com
books@bvks.com

First Edition, 2017: 1,000 copies

Published by Bhakti Vikas Trust, Surat, India.

Printed in India

Contents

Foreword

As if influenced by the worldwide dominance of *śūdra* culture, very few Gauḍīya Vaiṣṇavas today have even an inkling of the tremendous scholarly heritage to which they are heirs. And even if informed of it, very few take interest, as if it has nothing to do with them. But factually, service to the literary contributions of the previous *ācāryas* is a major area of devotional service that if neglected by the whole Vaiṣṇava community constitutes a collective offense known as *guror avajñā,* neglecting the gurus.

There is practically unlimited work to do in collecting, preserving, reproducing, translating, and commenting on old manuscripts, and in many other scholarly fields also. It is regrettable that much of the Vaiṣṇava world today is more inclined toward adapting Kṛṣṇa consciousness to *mleccha* society rather than understanding and embracing our own glorious and fully spiritual tradition.

Symptomatic of this is that despite the ongoing massive recruitment achievements of Śrīla A.C. Bhaktivedanta Swami Prabhupāda and his followers, only a very few within his community have shown serious interest in Vaiṣṇava scholarship – and most of those few have opted to pander to the largely agnostic secular academia. Hence appreciation is due to Bhakta Demian

(Dr. Demian Martins) for dedicating his life to one major area of research—the legacy of Gauḍīya Vedāntācārya Śrīla Baladeva Vidyābhūṣaṇa—which he is conducting in the straightforward traditional manner of a committed devotee, shunning the pretensions and prejudices of secular academia.

From my own dabblings in scholarly research, I came to learn what probably all serious researchers have experienced: sometimes while exploring in one area, one stumbles across another huge field of investigation in related or sometimes even distant topics. Thus it is that Bhakta Demian has taken an aside from his life's focus on Śrīla Baladeva Vidyābhūṣaṇa to publish this important book, which brings to light some largely unknown writings of Śrīla Prabodhānanda Sarasvatī.

Particularly valuable herein is Bhakta Demian's research and analysis concerning the identity of Śrīla Prabodhānanda Sarasvatī, which sheds new light on a long-standing controversy by making clear that the contention of certain polemicists has very little credibility. Followers of Śrīla Bhaktisiddhānta Sarasvatī Ṭhākura glorify him as *rūpānuga-viruddhāpasiddhānta-dhvānta-hārī,* "the remover of the darkness of faulty conclusions that oppose those of the followers of Śrīla Rūpa Gosvāmī" – which he did by establishing *sat-siddhānta* (proper philosophical conclusions), down to the minutest detail. It is in this tradition that Bhakta Demian has compiled this book, and naturally in doing so he also glorifies Śrīla

Prabodhānanda Sarasvatī and the subsequent *ācāryas* who have glorified him.

Śrīla Prabodhānanda Sarasvatī's poetic adoration of Śrī Caitanya Mahāprabhu, Śrī Rādhā, Śrī Vṛndāvana-dhāma, and Śrī Navadvīpa-dhāma, in his famous works *Śrī Rādhā-rasa-sudhā-nidhi, Śrī Caitanya-candrāmṛta, Vṛndāvana-śataka,* and *Navadvīpa-śataka,* is unprecedented in its unique ebullience. Among his other works are *Saṅgīta-Mādhava, Āścarya-rasa-prabandha, Śruti-stuti-vyākhyā, Gīta-govinda-vyākhyāna, Kāma-bīja-kāma-gāyatrī-vyākhyāna,* and a commentary on *Gopāla-tāpanī Upaniṣad.* The present book is actually a trilogy of Śrīla Prabodhānanda Sarasvatī's writings which were so far unknown to the public. In the longest of the three works, *Viveka-śatakam,* the author repeatedly expresses his ardent desire to go to Vṛndāvana. In *Caitanya-citrāṣṭakam* and *Nityānandāṣṭakam* he delightfully employs selected words of unalloyed ardour for his worshipable Lords. Typical of Śrīla Prabodhānanda Sarasvatī, his devotional ecstasy as if leaps from his heart into his words and therefrom to the heart of the sympathetic reader.

By traveling the length and breadth of India, often accepting very austere conditions in the course of undertaking perseverant, meticulous research, and by locating, translating, and publishing the manuscripts featured herein, Bhakta Demian has been able to perform this notable service of adding to the known canon of Śrīla Prabodhānanda Sarasvatī. All Gauḍīyas should be grateful to him for these contributions. May our *ācāryas* continue to bless him in his ongoing endeavours. We look forward to more such publications from him in the coming years.

Bhakti Vikāsa Swami

About the Author

By Śrīla Bhaktisiddhānta Sarasvatī[1]

In the beginning of the Śaka year of 1433 (1511 AD), on the pretext of a pilgrimage, Śrī Kṛṣṇa Caitanya Mahāprabhu distributed His mercy to the devotees. Starting in Nīlādri in Odisha, He first went to the Godāvarī confluence and then travelled through many holy places in the Madras area. On the Ekādaśī day of the bright fortnight of Āṣāḍha month, Śrīmān Mahāprabhu was present in Śrīraṅgam. Seeing that the Cāturmāsya period had arrived, Lord Caitanya decided to stay in Śrīraṅganātha Kṣetra to observe the rules and regulations pertaining to the *daśanāmi-sannyāsīs*. That was a residential place of the Śrī Vaiṣṇavas. The Vaiṣṇava *sampradāyas* in South India maintain strong faith in religious observances. In South India there are villages inhabited by transcendentalists who worship Lord Viṣṇu, and *smārta brāhmaṇas* overlook all inconveniences to live there. In those days, Śrīraṅgam was a holy place inhabited only by Śrī Vaiṣṇavas. Therefore, Śrīmān Mahāprabhu spent four months in the company of those virtuous Vaiṣṇavas, so surrendered and devoted to Lord Viṣṇu, and by having *darśana* of Lord Raṅganātha and preaching the transcendental topics on Lord Kṛṣṇa, He instructed the souls there. At that

1. This article was originally published as an introduction to the *Caitanya-candrāmṛta* and *Navadvīpa-śatakam*, Gauḍīya Maṭha, Kolkata, date unknown.

time, three brothers from Mysore had come to live in Śrīraṅgam. They were called Tirumalaya, Vyeṅkaṭa and Gopāla-guru (Prabodhānanda). Originally, they belonged either to Andhra Pradesh or Uttar Pradesh. Śrīmān Mahāprabhu was very pleased with this *brāhmaṇa* family and spent four months at their house. Vyeṅkaṭa was the middle brother, and his son, Gopāla Bhaṭṭa, who was then between five to ten years old, would later become one of the famous Gosvāmīs of Vṛndāvana.

The Śrī Vaiṣṇavas are mostly fond of worshipping Śrī Lakṣmī-Nārāyaṇa. By virtue of Śrīmān Mahāprabhu's special mercy, this Bhaṭṭa family became expert in relishing the *rasas* of Śrī Kṛṣṇa. Although we have no further information about Tirumalaya, it is understood that he was fully devoted to Lord Caitanya. The conversations between Lord Caitanya and Vyeṅkaṭa are described in the ninth chapter of the Madhya-līlā in the *Caitanya Caritāmṛta*. Prabodhānanda had an incomparable attachment for Lord Caitanya. It was by the influence of the instruction received from Prabodhānanda that Vyeṅkaṭa's son, Gopāla Bhaṭṭa, became an *ācārya* among the Gauḍīya Vaiṣṇavas. Prabodhānanda has a very elevated place among Lord Caitanya's servants. In his *Gaura-gaṇoddeśa-dīpikā*, verse 163, Kavi Karṇapūra has stated:

> *tuṅgavidyā vraje yāsīt sarva-śāstra-viśāradā*
> *sā prabodhānanda-yatir gaurodgāna-sarasvatī*

"She who was previously known in the pastimes of Kṛṣṇa in Vraja as Tuṅgavidyā, who is fully conversant with all scriptures, has now become Prabodhānanda Sarasvatī and is engaged in singing the glories of Lord Gaurāṅga."

In the beginning of the *Hari-bhakti-vilāsa* (1.2) it is stated:

bhakter vilāsāṁś cinute prabodhānandasya śiṣyo bhagavat-priyasya
gopāla-bhaṭṭo raghunātha-dāsaṁ santoṣayan rūpa-sanātanau ca

"Gopāla Bhaṭṭa, disciple of Śrīla Prabodhānanda, a dear associate of Lord Caitanya, is compiling this *Hari-bhakti-vilāsa* to please Śrīla Rūpa Gosvāmī, Śrīla Sanātana Gosvāmī and Śrīla Raghunātha Dāsa Gosvāmī."

In his *Bhakti-ratnākara* (1.149-150,152,153), Narahari Cakravartī says:

keha kahe prabodhānandera guṇa ati
sarvatra haila yāṁra khyāti sarasvatī

pūrṇa-brahma śrī-kṛṣṇa-caitanya bhagavān
tāṁra priya, tāṁra vinā svapane nāhi āna

parama-vairāgya-sneha mūrti manorama
mahā-kavi, gīta-vādya-nṛtya anupama

yāṁhāra vākya śuni' sukha bāḍaye sabāra
prabodhānandera mahā-mahimā apāra

"Some say that Prabodhānanda had many virtues. He became famous everywhere as 'Sarasvatī.' Even in dreams he did not know anyone else besides Śrī Kṛṣṇa Caitanya, the Supreme Brahman, Who was so dear to him. He was fascinating, supremely detached, affection personified, a great poet and incomparable in dance and music, both vocal and instrumental. He would increase the happiness of those who heard him speak. Prabodhānanda's glories are immense."

When Śrīmān Mahāprabhu returned to Nīlācala, in the subsequent years Prabodhānanda Sarasvatī became absorbed in intensely and wholeheartedly worshipping Him. Giving up Śrīraṅgam, He first took shelter of Lord Caitanya, and keeping in mind his desired mode of worship, without delay he went to live in Kāmyavana in the Mathurā district. Meanwhile, Gopāla Bhaṭṭa also gradually developed an intense desire to live in Vraja-dhāma and later followed in his uncle's footsteps.

Many people have a doubt regarding the reason for which Śrīla Kṛṣṇadāsa Kavirāja did not describe the glories of Śrīla Prabodhānanda Sarasvatī, although he was so dear to Lord Caitanya and although such topics give joy to his readers, the devotees of Lord Gaurāṅga. In reply to this, the statements penned in the *Bhakti-ratnākara* (209-211, 216, 222-224) are enough. There, Narahari Cakravartī says:

śrī-gopāla-bhaṭṭera e-saba vivaraṇa
keha kichu varṇe, keha nā kare varṇana

nā bujhiyā marma ithe kutarka ye kare
aparādha-bīja tāra hṛdaye sañcāre

parama-rasika pūrva pūrva kavi-gaṇa
varṇite samartha haiyā nā kare varṇana

rākhilena madhye madhye varṇana karite
varṇibe ye kavi-gaṇa tāṁhāra nimitte

śrī-gopāla-bhaṭṭa hṛṣṭa haiyā ājñā dila
granthe nija-prasaṅga varṇite niṣedhila

kene niṣedhila, ihā ke bujhite pāre?
nirantara atidīna māne āpanāre

kavirāja tāṁra ājñā nāre laṅghibāre
nāma-mātra likhe anya na kare pracāre

"Some authors have described the above-mentioned virtues of Śrīla Gopāla Bhaṭṭa to some extent, while others have not described them at all. Without understanding the reason behind it, some people indulge in flawed logic and thus the seed of offense sprouts in their hearts. Although fully capable to do it, the great *rasika* poets of the past did not describe much of his glories. Kṛṣṇadāsa Kavirāja Gosvāmī elaborately described the pastimes that were not described by Vṛndāvana dāsa Ṭhākura, but he also left some pastimes to be described by future poets. Feeling delighted upon receiving the order from many Vaiṣṇavas, Kṛṣṇadāsa Kavirāja Gosvāmī described the pastimes of Lord Mahāprabhu and His devotees in the *Caitanya-caritāmṛta*. Śrīla Gopāla Bhaṭṭa was also pleased to instruct Kṛṣṇadāsa to write the book, but forbade him to write about him (Gopāla Bhaṭṭa). Who can understand why he forbade him? He always considered himself very low. Śrīla Kavirāja Gosvāmī would not violate his order, therefore he only mentioned his name without describing his glories."

Some say that in the writings of Prabodhānanda Sarasvatī it is seen that he supports *svakīya-vāda* (the view that

Rādhā and Kṛṣṇa are a married couple), and therefore, observing the prominence of the *parakīya* (paramour) mode of worship among the Rūpānuga Vaiṣṇavas, he did not study much of the Gosvāmīs' works. However, devotees like Śrīla Narahari Cakravartī who are impartial and exclusively surrendered unto the lotus feet of Lord Caitanya are most fortunate. Therefore, like him, everyone should give up flawed logic and constantly relish the spotless way that Śrīla Prabodhānanda followed Lord Gaurāṅga and the sweetness of serving Śrī Vṛndāvaneśvarī in the *parakīya* mode.

Śrīla Prabodhānanda's mood is very clear, his language is deep and the presence of the *mādhurya* (mellow of conjugal love) mode is perceived at once. All Vaiṣṇavas surrendered at Lord Caitanya's feet attain incomparable joy by regularly reading Prabodhānanda's *Vṛndāvana-śatakam*. Similar to it is another book called *Navadvīpa-śatakam*. His poetical work *Rādhā-rasa-sudhānidhi* is indeed matchless in this world. Although by reading it one who is found of ordinary poetry will not derive much happiness, this book is very dear to the sincere devotees who are attached to the transcendental mellows of Lord Hari. There is an increase or diminution of excellence proportional to the level of taste, therefore the moods of the transcendental *rasas* of Vraja act over the readers according to their virtuous merit.

One other book of his is called *Viveka-śatakam*, whose description is found in Professor Aufrecht's catalogue and was seen by the late Rāmadāsa Sena from Behrampur. The book *Caitanya-candrāmṛta* is very popular in Bengal. Those who oppose Lord Gaurāṅga can have their minds purified by reading this. Needless to say, by reading it, Lord Gaurāṅga's devotees become absorbed in an indescribable ocean of transcendental bliss. During four months, the Lord of Goloka, Who is the very object of worship, distributed the rarely attained *kṛṣṇa-prema,* and the insignificant living entities around certainly hoped to obtain at least a portion of that imperishable and priceless reservoir.

Some people try to establish that the *māyāvādī* resident of Kāśī named Prakāśānanda and the great Vaiṣṇava named Prabodhānanda are the same person. However, we cannot believe in such an opinion because in connection with Prakāśānanda, the *māyāvādī* resident of Kāśī, the *Caitanya-bhāgavata* (Madhya, 3.3,18,35-40) states the following:

ei rūpe navadvīpe prabhu viśvambhara
bhakti-sukhe bhāse lai' sarva-anucara

eka-dina varāha-bhāvera śloka śuni
garjiyā murāri-ghare calilā āpani

gupta-vākye tuṣṭa hai' varāha-īśvara
veda-prati krodha kari' balaye uttara

hasta, pāda, mukha mora nāhika locana
vede more ei mata kare viḍambana

kāśīte paḍāya beṭā prakāśa-ānanda
sei beṭā kare mora aṅga khaṇḍa khaṇḍa

vākhānaye veda mora vigraha nā māne
sarvāṅge haila kuṣṭha, tabu nāhi jāne

sarva-yajña-maya mora ye aṅga pavitra
aja-bhava-ādi gāya yāṁhāra caritra

puṇya pavitratā pāya ye aṅga-paraśe
tāhā 'mithyā' bale beṭā kemana sāhase

"In this way, Lord Viśvambhara was floating in the ocean of devotional happiness in the company of His associates. One day, after hearing a verse about the mood of Lord Varāha, He roared loudly and went to the house of Murāri Gupta. Lord Caitanya in the mood of Varāha was pleased with Murāri Gupta's words. Displaying anger towards the Vedas, He replied, 'The Vedas deride Me by stating that I have no hands, legs, mouth or eyes. There is a rascal in Kāśī named Prakāśānanda, who in name of teaching the Vedas cuts My body into pieces. The rascal explains the Vedas but does not accept My form. His whole body is afflicted with leprosy, but even thus he does not understand. My sacred body is composed of all sacrifices. Even Lord Brahmā, Lord Śiva and other demigods sing its transcendental activities. By the touch of My body, virtue itself is purified, so how dare that rascal call it false?"

This incident happened between the Śaka years of 1425 (1503 AD) and 1430 (1508 AD). Śrīmān Mahāprabhu arrived in Śrīraṅgam in the Śaka year of 1433 (1511 AD) and met Prabodhānanda and his two brothers. At that time, they were Śrī Vaiṣṇavas, followers of Śrī Rāmānujācārya, and therefore they were *viśiṣṭādvaitavādīs*, always engaged in the service of Lord Nārāyaṇa's deity. On the other hand, Prakāśānanda was then a leading follower of the *māyāvāda* school established by Śaṅkara. To attempt to make these two individuals a single one is simply madness.

In connection with Prakāśānanda, the *Caitanya-bhāgavata* (Madhya, 20.32-36,40-41,44) describes the following:

balite prabhura haila īśvara āveśa
danta kaḍamaḍa kari' balaye viśeṣa

"sannyāsī prakāśānanda vasaye kāśīte
more khaṇḍa khaṇḍa beṭā kare bhāla mate

paḍāya vedānta, mora vigraha nā māne
kuṣṭha karāilum aṅge tabu nāhi jāne

ananta brahmāṇḍa mora ye aṅgete vaise
tāhā mithyā bale beṭā kemana sāhase?

satya kahoṁ, murāri, āmāra tumi dāsa
ye nā māne mora aṅga, sei yāya nāśa

satya mora līlā-karma, satya mora sthāna
ihā mithyā bale, more kare khāna khāna

ye yaśaḥ-śravaṇe āji avidyā-vināśa
pāpī adhyāpake bale 'mithyā se vilāsa'

hena puṇya-kīrti-prati anādara yāra
se kabhu nā jāne gupta mora avatāra

"Speaking thus, the Lord assumed the mood of the Supreme Controller. Grinding His teeth, He spoke something peculiar, 'A *sannyāsī* named Prakāśānanda resides in Kāśī. That rascal joyfully cuts Me into pieces. He teaches Vedānta but does not accept My form. I made him get leprosy, but even thus he does not understand. Unlimited universes rest within My body, so how dare that rascal call it false? O Murāri, I am telling you the truth because you are My servant. One who does not accept My form is doomed. My pastimes and activities are real and My abode is real. One who says that they are false cuts Me into pieces. By hearing My glories, all ignorance is destroyed. Yet sinful teachers say that My pastimes are false. O Murāri, one who disregards My auspicious glories can never understand My incarnation."

Prakāśānanda was then a leader of the *eka-daṇḍi-sannyāsīs* of the Śaṅkara-sampradāya in Kāśī, while Prabodhānanda had come from Mysore to live in Śrīraṅgam and was a *tri-daṇḍi-jīyāra-svāmī* follower of Rāmānujācārya. Prakāśānanda was a *māyāvādī* resident of Kāśī, and Prabodhānanda was a Vaiṣṇava who went to live in Kāmyavana. One lived in Āryavarta (North India), and the other was a South Indian Vaiṣṇava; one was an impersonalist, and the other was a personalist follower of *viśiṣṭādvaita*, and later of *acintya-bhedābheda*; one was opposed to Lord Viṣṇu and the Vaiṣṇavas who attained redemption, and he later became a devotee, while the other was a *nitya-siddha* associate of Lord Gaurāṅga and was the guru of Śrīla Gopāla Bhaṭṭa Gosvāmī. To deny that the worshipable uncle and guru of Gopāla Bhaṭṭa Gosvāmī was the best amongst eternally liberated devotees, and to insult and condemn him as a conditioned soul and *māyāvādī* who was inimical towards Lord Viṣṇu and the Vaiṣṇavas is an abominable Vaiṣṇava offense which will lead one to hell.

In the *Caitanya-caritāmṛta* (*Madhya*, chapter 25 and *Ādi*, 7.62 onwards) we find narrations about the *māyāvādī* Prakāśānanda. How a person who was a *māyāvādī* between the Śaka year of 1425 and 1430 (1503-1508 AD) could have gone to the South and become a Śrī Vaiṣṇava in 1433 (1511 AD), and then again become a *māyāvādī* in Kāśī in 1435 (1513 AD) cannot be understood. Therefore, the attempt to establish that Prakāśānanda and Prabodhānanda are the same person is a sign of utter ignorance. Consequently, this tendency to ruin historical facts in such a way causes great sadness. Being subjected to his own humbleness and meekness, Śrīla Prabodhānanda Sarasvatī had Śrīla Gopāla Bhaṭṭa forbid any narrations about him to be recorded in the *Caitanya-caritāmṛta*, and Śrīla Kavirāja Gosvāmī did not violate his order. Thus, we find the present difficulties. If Śrīla Prabodhānanda knew that in the future there would be a misleading attempt to include him amongst the class of offenders towards Lord Viṣṇu and the Vaiṣṇavas, then he would not have made such a prohibition. The readers of the *Bhakti-ratnākara* can understand this. In connection with Śrīla Prabodhānanda, in the *Bhakti-ratnākara* (1.83-84,128-129,133,135,149-150) it is written:

> *tirumalaya, vyeṅkaṭa, āra prabodhānanda*
> *tina bhrātāra prāṇa-dhana gauracandra*

lakṣmī-nārāyana-upāsaka e tina pūrvate
rādhā-kṛṣṇa-rase matta prabhura kṛpāte

tirumalaya, vyeṅkaṭa, prabodhānanda tine
vicāraye – prabhu vine rahiba kemane?

mo-sabara saṅge parihāsa ke karibe?
kāverī-snānete saṅge kebā lañā yābe?

cārimāsa pare prabhu hailā vidāya
tina bhāi krandana karaye ubharāya

prabhu tina bhrātāya kari' āliṅgana
kahilā aneka-rūpa prabodha-vacana

keha kahe prabodhānandera guṇa ati
sarvatra haila khyāti yati 'sarasvatī'

pūrṇa-brahma śrī-kṛṣṇa-caitanya bhagavān
tāṁra priya, tāṁra vinā svapane nāhi āna

"Lord Gauracandra was the life and soul of these three brothers, namely Tirumalaya, Vyeṅkaṭa and Prabodhānanda. They were previously worshippers of Lakṣmī-Nārāyaṇa, but by the mercy of Lord Caitanya they became mad for the mellows of Rādhā-Kṛṣṇa. At the imminence of the Lord's departure, these three brothers thought, 'How can we remain without the Lord? Who will cut jokes with us? Who will accompany us to bathe in the River Kāverī?' After four months, Lord Caitanya bade farewell and the brothers started crying loudly. The Lord then embraced the three brothers and spoke some words to console them. Some say that Prabodhānanda had many virtues. He became famous everywhere as

'Sarasvatī.' Even in dreams he did not know anyone else besides Śrī Kṛṣṇa Caitanya, the Supreme Brahman, Who was so dear to him."

In the catalogue of Professor Aufretch, a book named *Saṅgīta-Mādhava* was also classified as a work of Śrīla Prabodhānanda Sarasvatī. We have collected this book and it was fully published in the magazine *Sajjana-toṣaṇī*, 18th year, from issues 5 to 12.

The householder Vaiṣṇavas in the Śrī-sampradāya do not give up family life to take *eka-daṇḍa-sannyāsa.* In that line, all renunciants take *'tri-daṇḍa-sannyāsa'* and are known as *'Śrī-Rāmānujīya Svāmīs.'* Having analyzed Śrīla Prabodhānanda's *Caitanya-candrāmṛta*, some conclude that he was an impersonalist *sannyāsī.* However, by accepting this view in the absence of clear evidence, many difficulties will appear.

Introduction

According to several accounts, Śrīla Prabodhānanda Sarasvatī was a dear associate of Lord Caitanya Mahāprabhu and was also one of the pioneers in praising His glories in Sanskrit poetry in his book named *Caitanya-candrāmṛta.* At the same time, his figure is one of the most controversial among the Gauḍīyas. The utter silence of Śrīla Kṛṣṇadāsa Kavirāja and Śrīla Vṛndāvanadāsa Ṭhākura about Prabodhānanda led to different conjectures, and the conflicting narrations of later Gauḍīya hagiographers overshadowed him in a cloud of mystery and confusion. We find no date of his birth, demise, travels or any incident of his life, about which there is hardly anything known, apart from whatever is mentioned in his own writings and the terse verses of a few other authors. Furthermore, none of the works attributed to Prabodhānanda seem to have ever been quoted by his contemporaries or other Gauḍīyas until the 18th century. Most of his writings were unknown until they started to be published in late 19th century. In particular, two controversies have been prevalent for over a century – his alleged past as a *māyāvādī sannyāsī* in Vārāṇasī under the name 'Prakāśānanda Sarasvatī,' and his supposed relation with Śrī Hita Harivaṁśa, founder of the Rādhā-vallabha-sampradāya. In order to establish a plausible conclusion, it is commendable to first go through an overview of the available data and assess its integrity. What follows comprises most of the statements about Prabodhānanda Sarasvatī made by notable authors between the 16th and the 18th centuries.

From his own statement, we know that Gopāla Bhaṭṭa Gosvāmī was a disciple of Prabodhānanda Sarasvatī, the only one we hear of, although it is not clear whether he was his *śikṣā-guru, dīkṣā-guru* or both. From other sources we also hear that they had a blood connection as uncle and nephew. Yet in the works attributed to Gopāla Bhaṭṭa, Prabodhānanda's name is mentioned only once. At the beginning of the *Hari-bhakti-vilāsa* (1.2) it is written:

bhakter vilāsāṁś cinute prabodhānandasya śiṣyo bhagavat-priyasya gopāla-bhaṭṭo raghunātha-dāsaṁ santoṣayan rūpa-sanātanau ca

"Gopāla Bhaṭṭa, disciple of Śrīla Prabodhānanda, a dear associate of Lord Caitanya, is compiling this *Hari-bhakti-vilāsa* to please Śrīla Rūpa Gosvāmī, Śrīla Sanātana Gosvāmī and Śrīla Raghunātha Dāsa Gosvāmī."

In the commentary attributed to Śrīla Sanātana Gosvāmī it is stated:

bhagavat-priyasyeti bahuvrīhiṇā tatpuruṣeṇa vā samāsena tasya māhātmya-jātaṁ pratipāditam | evaṁ tac-chiṣyasya śrī-gopāla-bhaṭṭasyāpi tādṛktvaṁ boddhavyam |

"By the words *bhagavat-priyasya*, which can be interpreted either as a *bahuvrīhi* compound (*to whom Lord Caitanya is very dear*) or as a *tatpuruṣa* compound (*who is very dear to Lord Caitanya*), Śrī Prabodhānanda's glories are expressed.

In the same way, the glories of his disciple, Śrī Gopāla Bhaṭṭa, are understood to be similar to his."

In the *Gaura-gaṇoddeśa-dīpikā,* Kavi Karṇapūra enumerated the main associates of Lord Caitanya and their respective identities in *kṛṣṇa-līlā.* In verse 163 he says:

tuṅgavidyā vraje yāsīt sarva-śāstra-viśāradā
sā prabodhānanda-yatir gaurodgāna-sarasvatī

"She who was previously known in the pastimes of Kṛṣṇa in Vraja as Tuṅgavidyā, who is fully conversant with all scriptures, has now become Prabodhānanda Sarasvatī and is engaged in singing the glories of Lord Gaurāṅga."

As Prabodhānanda is identified as one of the main eight *gopīs* of Vraja, it is understood that such an intimate associate must have played an essential role in *caitanya-līlā.* From the statements of Sanātana Gosvāmī and Karṇapūra it is implied that Prabodhānanda had the association of Lord Caitanya at some point of life. Since we find no descriptions of their meeting in Navadvīpa or Purī, the most obvious conclusion is that they spent four months together in Śrīraṅgam during the Lord's South Indian tour, as pointed out by the texts quoted below. There are no other instances of the Lord spending so much time in a family's house, which means the Bhaṭṭa family was very special and dear to Him. By the name 'Tuṅgavidyā' (*she who has exalted knowledge*) we can also understand that Prabodhānanda was conversant with spiritual knowledge, which he imparted to his disciple Gopāla, who subsequently became the main initiator spiritual master in Vṛndāvana. From these two perspectives, Prabodhānanda holds indeed a very distinguished position in the pastimes of Lord Caitanya.

At the end of his commentary on the *Gopāla-tāpany-upaniṣad,* Śrīla Jīva Gosvāmī states:

> *viśveśvaraka-janārdana-bhaṭṭābhyāṁ vaidikācāryābhyām |*
> *tadvat prabodha-yatinā likhitaṁ citram atra tāratamyena ||*
>
> *śrī-sanātana-rūpasya caraṇābja-sudhepsunā |*
> *pūritā ṭippaṇī ceyaṁ jīvena sukha-bodhinī ||*

"Previously, the Vedic preceptors named Viśveśvara and Janārdana Bhaṭṭa, as well as the *sannyāsī* Prabodha have written commentaries on this text, each more interesting than the previous one. Now this commentary called *Sukha-bodhinī* has been completed by Jīva, desiring to obtain the nectarean water from the feet of Śrīla Rūpa and Śrīla Sanātana Gosvāmīs."

There is a work attributed to Jīva Gosvāmī named *Vaiṣṇava-vandanā,* where we find the following verse (71) :

> *prabodhānanda-sarasvatīṁ vande vimalāṁ yayā mudā |*
> *candrāmṛtaṁ racitaṁ yac-chiṣyo gopāla-bhaṭṭakaḥ ||*

"I offer my humble obeisances unto the spotless Śrīla Prabodhānanda Sarasvatī, who joyfully compiled the *Caitanya-candrāmṛta,* and whose disciple is Śrīla Gopāla Bhaṭṭa Gosvāmī."

In the compilation *Vyāsajī kī Vāṇī,* we find the following verses by Harirāma Vyāsa (16th century):

prabodhānanda se kavi thore

jina rādhā-vallabha kī līlā-rasa me saba rasa ghore |
kevala prema-vilāsa āsa kari, bhava-bandhana dṛḍha tore ||

sahaja mādhurī vacanani, rasika ananyani ke cita core |
pāvana rūpa-nāma-guṇa ura dhari, viṣai-vikāra ju more ||

cāru caraṇa-nakha-canda-bimba meṁ rākhe naina cakore |
jāyā, māyā, gṛha, dehī soṁ, ravi-suta bandhana chore ||

"Poets like Prabodhānanda are very rare. He sang about all mellows in the divine pastimes of Rādhā and Kṛṣṇa. Having broken the strong bounds of material life, his only hope was to relish those loving pastimes. His natural, sweet words stole the minds of other exclusively devoted *rasikas*. Inside his heart, he always held the Lord's pure qualities, names and forms and thus turned away from all sensual agitation. Like a *cakora* bird, he kept his eyes on the moon-like reflection of the beautiful nails of the Lord's feet and in this way gave up illusory happiness, wife, home, the bodily conception and the grip of Yamarāja."

In his *Vaiṣṇava-vandanā,* Devakīnandana[2] writes:

prabodhānanda gosāñi vandoṁ kariyā yatana
ye karilā mahāprabhura guṇera varṇana

"I eagerly offer obeisances unto Śrīla Prabodhānanda Gosvāmī, who described the transcendental qualities of Lord Caitanya Mahāprabhu."

---

2. Also called Daivakīnandana. He was a disciple of Puruṣottama, a disciple of Nityānanda Prabhu.

In his *Vaiṣṇava-vandanā*, Vṛndāvanadāsa[3] writes:

vandoṁ kariyā bhakti, prabodhānanda sarasvatī, parama mahattva guṇa-dhāma | śrī-caitanya-candrāmṛta pustaka yāṁhāra kṛta, ei pūnthi bhakta-dhana-prāṇa ||

"With great devotion I offer obeisances to Śrīla Prabodhānanda Sarasvatī, who is an abode of transcendental qualities and greatness. He composed the book *Śrī-Caitanya-candrāmṛta,* which is the devotees' treasure and life."

In the *Sādhana-dīpikā* (*Aṣṭama-kakṣā*), Rādhā-Kṛṣṇa Gosvāmī[4] states:

śrīmat-prabodhānandasya bhrātuḥ putraṁ kṛpālayam |
śrīmad-gopāla-bhaṭṭaṁ taṁ naumi śrī-vraja-vāsinam ||

"I offer my humble obeisances unto Śrīla Gopāla Bhaṭṭa, who was the son of Śrīla Prabodhānanda's brother, a resident of Vraja and a reservoir of mercy."

In the first chapter of the *Anurāgavallī* (dated 1696 AD), Manohara Dāsa[5] writes:

---

3. This is not the author of *Caitanya-bhāgavata.* In the *Karṇānanda,* Yadunandana dāsa mentions two devotees with this name – one was a son and the other was a disciple of Śrīnivāsācarya (17th century AD).

4. He was a *pujārī* in the Govindadeva Mandira in the 17th century. His guru was Haridāsa Paṇḍita, *sevādhikārī* of the temple and a disciple of Anantācārya, a disciple of Gadādhara Paṇḍita. Vide *Caitanya-caritāmṛta,* Ādi-līlā, 8.54-65.

5. He was a disciple of Śrī Rāmaśaraṇa Caṭṭarāja, who was the

sei tīrthe vaise tailaṅga-viprarāja |
śrī-trimalla-bhaṭṭa nāma brāhmaṇa-samāja ||

tāṁhāra kaniṣṭha jyeṣṭha haye dui bhāi |
veṅkaṭa prabodhānanda bhaṭṭa bali gāi ||

veṅkaṭera kaniṣṭha prabodhānanda nāma |
gopāla-bhaṭṭera pūrve guru se pramāṇa ||

adhyayana upanayana yogya ācaraṇe |
pūrvate sakala śikṣā pitṛvyera sthāne ||

"In that holy place, Śrīraṅgam, lived Trimalla Bhaṭṭa, the best in the Tailaṅga *brāhmaṇa* community. He had an older and a younger brother named Veṅkaṭa Bhaṭṭa and Prabodhānanda Bhaṭṭa. Veṅkaṭa Bhaṭṭa's younger brother was named Prabodhānanda, who was the first guru of Gopāla Bhaṭṭa according to his own testimony. By his good conduct, Gopāla Bhaṭṭa was qualified for studying the scriptures and receiving the sacred thread. He formerly received his whole education in the house of his uncle."

In the *Bhakta-māla* (paragraph 182), Nābhājī (16th- 17th century AD) refers to Prabodhānanda in the following words:

prabodhānanda, rāmabhadra, jagadānanda kali-jugga dhani
parama-dharma prati poṣakauṁ, sannyāsī e mukuṭamani

son of Śrī Kṛṣṇadāsa Caṭṭarāja and a disciple of Śrī Rāmacaraṇa Cakravartī, both disciples of Śrīnivāsācārya, who was a disciple of Śrīla Gopāla Bhaṭṭa Gosvāmī.

"Prabodhānanda, Rāmabhadra and Jagadānanda made Kali-yuga blessed. They were the crest jewels among *sannyāsīs* and maintained the highest religious principles."

In the commentary (dated 1712 AD) to the above paragraph, Priyādāsa[6] says:

śrī-prabodhānanda baḍe rasika ānanda-kanda śrī-caitanya-canda jū ke pārakhada pyāre haiṁ | rādhā-kṛṣṇa-kuñja-keli, nipaṭa naveli kahī, jheli rasa-rūpa, doū kie dṛg tāre haiṁ || vṛndāvana vāsa kau hulāsa lai prakāśa kiyau, diyau sukha-sindhu, karma dharma saba ṭāre haiṁ | tāhī suni suni koṭi koṭi jana raṅga pāyo, vipina suhāyau vase tana mana cāre haiṁ ||

"Śrīla Prabodhānanda was a great *rasika* and a beloved associate of Lord Caitanya, bliss personified. He gave fresh descriptions of the amorous pastimes of Śrī Śrī Rādhā and Kṛṣṇa in the groves of Vraja. He relished Their forms and *rasas* and made Them his dearmost. In his poems, he revealed the splendour of residing in Śrī Vṛndāvana and thus merged the devotees in an ocean of happiness. He became aloof from all materially motivated activities and religiosity. Listening to his poems, millions of people fell in love. While residing himself in the beautiful Vṛndāvana, he sacrificed his body and mind in Their service."

In the first chapter of the *Bhakti-ratnākara,* Narahari Cakravartī[7] says:

6. He was a disciple of Manohara dāsa.

7. He lived in the first half of the 18th century and belonged to the disciplic succession coming down from Gopāla Bhaṭṭa

saṁkṣepe kahile ethā bhaṭṭa-vivaraṇa |
śrī-gopāla-bhaṭṭa hana vyeṅkaṭa-nandana || 81 ||

trimalla, vyeṅkaṭa āra śrī-prabodhānanda |
e tina bhrātāra prāṇa-dhana gauracandra || 83 ||

gaura-guṇa-mahimā ye sarvatra prakāśe |
māyāvāda-khaṇḍana karaye anāyāse || 145 ||

gopāla-bhaṭṭera ślāghā kare śiṣṭa-gaṇa |
kirūpe karila aiche vidyā-upārjana || 146 ||

keha kahe śrī-prabodhānanda yatna kaila |
alpa-kāla haite adhyayana karāila || 147 ||

pitṛvya-kṛpāya sarva-śāstre haila jñāna |
gopālera sama ethā nāi vidyāvān || 148 ||

keha kahe prabodhānandera guṇa ati |
sarvatra haila yāṁra khyāti sarasvatī|| 149 ||

pūrṇa-brahma śrī-kṛṣṇa-caitanya bhagavān |
tāṁra priya, tāṁra vinā svapane nāhi āna || 150 ||

parama-vairāgya-sneha mūrti manorama |
mahā-kavi, gīta-vādya-nṛtya anupama || 152 ||

yāṁhāra vākya śuni' sukha bāḍaye sabāra |
prabodhānandera mahā-mahimā apāra || 153 ||

prabodhānandera bhrātuṣputra śrī-gopāla |
sarva-mate suśikṣita parama dayāla || 155 ||

"I will now briefly describe the Bhaṭṭa family. Śrī Gopāla Bhaṭṭa was the son of Śrī Veṅkaṭa Bhaṭṭa. Lord Gauracandra

---

Gosvāmī and Śrīnivāsācārya.

was the life and treasure of the three brothers, Trimalla, Veṅkaṭa and Prabodhānanda. Śrī Gopāla Bhaṭṭa revealed the glories and transcendental qualities of Lord Gaurāṅga everywhere and would easily defeat *māyāvāda* arguments. Even learned scholars praised Gopāla Bhaṭṭa. How had he acquired such knowledge? Some say that this was all due to the efforts of Śrī Prabodhānanda, who taught him in a very short time. By his uncle's mercy, he obtained knowledge of all scriptures. There is no learned man like Gopāla Bhaṭṭa in this world. Some say that Prabodhānanda had many virtues. He became famous everywhere as 'Sarasvatī.' Even in dreams he did not know anyone else besides Śrī Kṛṣṇa Caitanya, the Supreme Brahman, Who was so dear to him. He was fascinating, supremely detached, affection personified, a great poet and incomparable in dance and music, both vocal and instrumental. He would increase the happiness of those who heard him speak. Prabodhānanda's glories are immense. In the opinion of everyone, Gopāla Bhaṭṭa, the son of Prabodhānanda's brother, was very well educated and very kind."

Up to this point there is no controversy, except for one issue mentioned by Manohara Dāsa that in the *Caitanya-caritāmṛta, Madhya-līlā* 1.108 it is stated that Mahāprabhu stayed at the house of Trimalla Bhaṭṭa, while in the *Madhya-līlā* 9.82 and subsequent verses it is stated that He was taken to Veṅkaṭa Bhaṭṭa's house. This is a minor issue that can be easily solved by assuming that the brothers lived in the same house. Yet it seems that for this reason some authors described either Trimalla or Veṅkaṭa as the eldest and the father of Gopāla Bhaṭṭa. In this regard, it is also interesting to note that the present descendants of this family in Śrīraṅgam, headed by Śrī Muralī Bhaṭṭar, do not have any information or records of a third brother called Prabodha or Prabodhānanda. This could be due to several factors, such as the extinction of his lineage or the migration of his descendants to a distant region, which within the time frame of five centuries could not be easily traced. It is also possible that Prabodhānanda was a cousin-brother or a distant relative of the same generation and was therefore affectionately considered a brother in the family.

From the above verses it is crystal clear that none of these respectable authors ever gave the slightest hint that Prabodhānanda might have been anyone else but a South Indian Vaiṣṇava and the instructor of Gopāla Bhaṭṭa. It is thus also understood that the idea that he was a *māyāvādī sannyāsī* in Vārāṇasī was a much later misunderstanding perpetrated by texts written by doubtful authors. If there were any apprehension in this regard in the days of Narahari Cakravartī and Manohara Dāsa, they would surely have addressed it in their works, where they did not hesitate to deal with several other controversies. This means that this only became an issue subsequently. One of the earliest authors responsible for this misconception is Ānandī, who wrote the first known Sanskrit commentary (dated 1723 AD) on the *Caitanya-candrāmṛta,* which starts with the following words:

śrī-śrīpāda-parivrāja-rājovedānta-sāṅkhya-vaiśeṣika-pātañjala-mīmāṁsāgama-nigama-mahā-purāṇa-purāṇa-setihāsa-pañcarātrālaṅkāra-kāvya-nāṭakādi-rahasya-siddhāntānargala-vaktṛtvojjvalī-kṛtāsaṅkhya-kāśī-vāsy-antevāsika-janānām antaḥ-karaṇakaḥ |

"Śrīla Prabodhānanda Sarasvatī was the king of the itinerant mendicants in the renounced order and was very dear to innumerable students who lived in Kāśī and shined by their fluent eloquence in the secret conclusions of many subject matters such as Vedānta, Sāṅkhya, Vaiśeṣika, Pātañjala yoga, Mīmāṁsā, Āgama, Nigama, Purāṇas, Mahāpurāṇas, itihāsas, Pañcarātra, rhetorics, poetry, dramaturgy, etc."

Nothing definite is known about Ānandī's lineage and background, so against the weight of all the previous authors, there is no reason to accept him as an authority regarding Prabodhānanda's life. Yet this single mistaken statement has misled future generations. He might have assumed that Prabodhānanda was a resident of Kāśī on the basis of verse 99 in the *Caitanya-candrāmṛta:*

> *kāśī-vāsīn api na gaṇaye kiṁ gayāṁ mārgayāmo*
> *muktiḥ śuktībhavati yadi me kaḥ parārtha-prasaṅgaḥ* |
>
> *trāsābhāsaḥ sphurati na mahā-raurave'pi kva bhītiḥ*
> *strī-putrādau yadi kṛpayate deva-devaḥ sa gauraḥ* ||

"If Lord Gaurāṅga, the Supreme God of all demigods, is merciful upon me, then I do not take into consideration even the residents of Kāśī. Why then should we visit Gayā to offer oblations to our ancestors? If Lord Gaurāṅga is merciful upon me, I consider *mukti* itself a trifle, so what to speak of *dharma, artha* and *kāma*? If Lord Gaurāṅga is merciful upon me, I do not have the slightest fear of even going to hell, so where is the question of fearing for my wife, sons and other relatives?"

Such an assumption, however, is not well thought, for the point the author is making here is that he considers the mercy of Lord Caitanya much higher than residence in Vārāṇasī, which is praised as a place where the residents attain liberation upon giving up their present body. This is confirmed in the next line, when he further states that he actually considers Mahaprabhu's mercy to be superior to even liberation itself.

The *Advaita-prakāśa* (17th chapter), attributed to Īśāna Nāgara, describes the supposed meeting of Lord Caitanya with Prabodhānanda in Vārāṇasī:

kāśī pūrṇa haila gorāra prabhāva-sambandhe |
aneka vaiṣṇava hailā sei anubandha ||

tathi śrī-prabodhānanda sarasvatī khyāti |
sannyāsīra madhye yiṁha buddhe bṛhaspati ||

bahu-śāstra-vettā paṇḍitera śikhāmaṇi |
gaurāṅga nindiye tiṁha hañā abhimānī ||

dayā-sindhu śrī-caitanya dayā prakāśilā |
bahu-śāstra-yuktyā tare svamate ānilā||

śrī-prabodhānandera saba khaṇḍila saṁśaya |
gaurāṅge īśvara bali karilā niścaya ||

śrī-prabodhānande horā baḍa dayā kailā |
śakti sañcāriyā tare prema-bhakti dilā ||

parama vaiṣṇava haila śrī-prabodhānanda |
khaṇḍila kutarka vāda pāila premānanda ||

sarasvatī hailā gaurera bhakata pravīṇa |
kṛta pīta rūpe prakaṭa kahe rātri dina ||

"By Lord Caitanya's transcendental power, Kāśī attained plenitude and many people became Vaiṣṇavas.

"Among the *sannyāsīs,* Prabodhānanda was famous like Sarasvatī and intelligent like Bṛhaspati. He knew so many scriptures and was the crest jewel among learned scholars. Thus becoming very proud, he indulged in criticizing Lord Gaurāṅga. Lord Caitanya is an ocean of mercy and therefore showed kindness to him. By debating with logic on the conclusion of the scriptures, He convinced him about His philosophy. Mahāprabhu removed all his doubts, and at last Prabodhānanda accepted Him as the Supreme Lord. Showing great mercy on Prabodhānanda, Lord Caitanya empowered him and gave him pure loving devotional service. Once his flawed arguments were defeated, Prabodhānanda became an exalted Vaiṣṇava and attained the bliss of love of God. He became a staunch devotee of Lord Caitanya and spent day and night saying that the Lord was Kṛṣṇa in a golden colour."

Īśāna Nāgara is said to have been a servant in Advaita Prabhu's house and supposedly wrote this book in 1568 AD. If it is true that such a person wrote *Advaita-prakāśa* in this year, then what has been passed down to our hands is an extensively interpolated version. While some accounts in *Advaita-prakāśa* seem to be legitimate and match with those found in other books, on the other hand there are several suspicious incidents which are not to be found anywhere else and others that clash with versions that are present within more reliable and widely accepted hagiographies. This undermines its credibility to a great extent, therefore some Gauḍīya scholars hold the opinion that *Advaita-prakāśa* is a much later compilation of someone else and was intentionally given a backdate. In fact, no ancient author has ever quoted it, and until the late 19th century its very name seemed to be unknown. The Catalogus Catalogorum of Bengali Manuscripts lists only two existent copies, which makes us wonder why those in Advaitācārya's line never took an interest in circulating this book if it is an authentic hagiography.

In the Bengali *Bhakta-māla,* Lāladāsa (18th century) declares:

> *prakāśānanda sarasvatī nāma chila |*
> *prabhura prabodhānanda baliyā rākhila ||*

"Mahāprabhu then changed the name of Prakāśānanda Sarasvatī into Prabodhānanda Sarasvatī."

This might be the first instance in which both are described as the same person. Originally meant to be a Bengali version of the Hindi *Bhakta-māla* with emphasis on the Gauḍīya devotees, the author could not refrain from adding many obscure episodes and descriptions without precedents. Despite Lāladāsa's claims that he is presenting the facts as they are, in many respects his compilation is so flawed that Śrīla Bhaktisiddhānta Sarasvatī referred to it as a *sahajiyā* book. Although very popular in West Bengal, this work has never earned the trust of historians and Gauḍīya scholars at large on account of several absurdities and anachronisms. It is apparent that many of the statements are rumours or mere concoctions – for example, the exchange of letters between Lord Caitanya and Prakāśānanda. Mahāprabhu did not usually change the names of His followers. Rūpa and Sanātana are the most well-known instances, and their change of name was well justified, since they were being addressed by Muslim names. However, in the case of Prakāśānanda (*the bliss of light*), there is hardly any improvement by changing his name into Prabodhānanda (*the bliss of awakening*). If the former name sounded too impersonal for a Vaiṣṇava, the new name did not sound any more devotional.

Shishir Kumar Ghosh (1840-1911), a famous Bengali journalist and founder of the *Amrita Bazar Patrika*, appreciated Lāladāsa's divagations so much that he wrote a hundred-page novel entitled *Śrī Prabodhānanda O Śrī Gopāla Bhaṭṭa,* which culminates with the metamorphosis of Prakāśānanda into Prabodhānanda. This book played a definite role in propagating the myth among the Bengali public, although it includes fanciful imaginary descriptions and lacks historical evidence or authentic sources to support the author's assumptions.

The advocates of the Prakāśānanda tale also owe us an explanation as to when and where he taught Gopāla Bhaṭṭa. Even the texts that support their claim totally omit this point. We hear from the *Bhakti-ratnākara* and other works that by the time Gopāla Bhaṭṭa left Śrīraṅgam and reached Vṛndāvana as a young man, he was already an accomplished scholar. Nowhere can we find descriptions of a *māyāvādī sannyāsī* coming from Kāśī to Śrīraṅgam to teach him. Furthermore, we hear from the *Bhakti-ratnākara* that Gopāla Bhaṭṭa could easily defeat *māyāvāda*, and this would not be possible if he had been educated by a *māyāvādī*. It is also unlikely that an exalted Vaiṣṇava like Gopāla Bhaṭṭa Gosvāmī would have been educated by a *māyāvādī*. The present descendants of the Bhaṭṭa family flatly deny such a possibility, for it is totally unprecedented that one of them would give up their spiritual lineage to join the Śaṅkara line. This would have demoralized the family, and by no means would they be able to still hold a prestigious position as leading priests in the Śrī Raṅganātha Temple as they do even today. No Śrī Vaiṣṇava would allow his children to be taught by a follower of Śaṅkara, what to speak of in Śrīraṅgam, the headquarters of the Śrī-sampradāya. Also, *sannyāsīs* do not visit householders in order to teach their children. To visit one's family's house is also completely against the code of conduct for a *sannyāsī*. Additionally, we do not find any description of Gopāla Bhaṭṭa going to Kāśī to study. If it be said that Prabodhānanda took *māyāvādī sannyāsa* after teaching Gopāla in Śrīraṅgam, then we have to ask how an obscure resident of South India would have become so popular in Vārāṇasī to have already secured thousands of disciples by the time Lord Caitanya arrived there in 1514 AD, just three years after his visit to Śrīraṅgam. We also know from different sources that Lord Caitanya could not tolerate *māyāvāda* at all, so why would he accept to stay four months with the family of a *māyāvādī*? On the contrary, the *Caitanya-bhāgavata* (*Madhya*, 3.3,18-40) tells us how even before taking *sannyāsa* and visiting South India, Mahāprabhu was already indignant due to the offenses committed by Prakāśānanda in Kāśī.

Some argue that 'Sarasvatī' is one of the ten titles (daśanāma) adopted by the *eka-daṇḍi-sannyāsīs* who belong to Śaṅkara's *sampradāya,* and that no Śrī Vaiṣṇava *tri-daṇḍi-sannyāsī* has ever adopted this name. Yet from the *Bhakti-ratnākara* it is clear that even before he became a renunciant, Prabodhānanda was already known as 'Sarasvatī' on account of his scholarship. Nowhere is it mentioned that this was his *sannyāsa* title.

From the *Gaura-gaṇoddeśa-dīpikā* we know that the prominent *gopīs* and *mañjarīs* appeared as companions of Mahāprabhu. We would also like to hear an explanation as to why Tuṅgavidyā, one of the *aṣṭa-sakhīs* in Vṛndāvana, would appear as a *māyāvādī* who became a leper for blaspheming the Lord, while all the other *nitya-siddhas* spent their lives serving and glorifying Him. Jagāi and Mādhāi were insignificant rogues in a village, yet their deliverance was sung far and wide by many contemporary Gauḍīya poets. How much greater an accomplishment would the conversion of the greatest *māyāvādī* scholar and guru of Vārāṇasī be and his turning into a *rasika* poet – yet everyone is silent about it! The simple explanation is that all contemporary authors knew very well that Prakāśānanda and Prabodhānanda were two completely distinct persons. The *Madhya-līlā* of the *Caitanya-caritāmṛta* ends with the description of how Prakāśānanda underwent a change of heart, regretted his offenses and surrendered at the feet of Lord Caitanya. Nowhere is it mentioned that he became a *rasika mahā-bhāgavata* and travelled to Vṛndāvana. Mahāprabhu returned to Purī, Tapana Miśra and Candraśekhara went to Vṛndāvana, and in the meantime we do not know of any Gauḍīya devotee that visited Vārāṇasī, thus there was no one to tell us what happened to Prakāśānanda. If he had left for Vṛndāvana, it would seem that a large contingent amongst his many thousands of disciples would have followed him there. The arrival of such a great scholar in Vṛndāvana accompanied by thousands of followers would certainly have been recorded in chronicles and poems. However, we hear nothing of the sort. As he was already an old man in poor health, most probably he spent the rest of his days in Vārāṇasī itself.

At this point, any sober reader will have already concluded that there is absolutely no possibility that Prabodhānanda and Prakāśānanda were one and the same, and that this confusion was propagated by misinformed later authors. On the other hand, the cause and the solution of their confusion may possibly be one and the same. For a long time, the Rādhā-vallabha Vaiṣṇavas have been aware that there are two Prabodhānandas in this discussion. One of the earliest evidences is Priyādāsa's *Bhakta-sumiranī,*[8] a list of devotees who lived in Vraja, where he mentions two persons with a similar name:

śrī-prabodha rasa-rāsa rasika vasa |
jyāye jiya de prema-sudhā-rasa || 69 ||
śrī-prabodha vimalānanda santa | 70 |

"Śrī Prabodha was the master among the *rasika* devotees expert in relishing all transcendental mellows and was therefore given the nectarean *rasa* of love for Kṛṣṇa. Śrī Prabodha was a saint absorbed in pure bliss."

śrī-prabodhānanda raṅgīna |
gāi kuñja-keli rasika pravīna || 118 ||

"Śrī Prabodhānanda was a very learned *rasika* who sang the loving pastimes performed in the groves of Vṛndāvana."

By the word play (Prabodha and *vimalānanda*) in verse 70, it may be implied that he could also be called Prabodhānanda, and to make it clear that there was a totally different person with the same name, the author mentioned the other one many verses later.

In the *Rasik Ananya Māl* (circa 1600 AD), a brief hagiography of thirty-four notable Vaiṣṇavas of the Rādhā-vallabha-sampradāya, Bhagavat Mudita gives the most extensive

8. At the Janmasthāna Śodha Pīṭha, Mathurā, there is a manuscript copy dated 1775 Saṁvat (1718 AD).

known description about the Prabodhānanda of that line as follows:

aba suni śrī harivaṁśa pada, gahyau prabodhānanda | pāyau nitya-vihāra sukha, tajyau su brahmānanda || prabodhānanda hute sannyāsī | jāke guru mata śūnya udāsī || dvitiya sarasvatī saba disi jītī | paṇḍita baḍe baḍe avinītī || kāśī se vṛndāvana āye | eka māsa rahi ati sukha pāye || sabahī ṭhākura dvāre dekhe | aur sabai ācāraja pekhe || saba ke mata nīke kari jāne | pai prabodha ke mana nahiṁ māne || paramānanda rasika kahuṁ mile | caracā karata duhuni mana khile || nita-vihāra kī caracā ṭhānī | so prabodha ke mana nahiṁ ānī || śruti-smṛti itihāsa sunāye | sanaka-saṁhitā ke mata gāye || āgama bāvana bṛhad purāna | inahiṁ ādi kahe bahut pramāna || tāmeṁ mānasarovara kahyau | nitya-vihāra rasika jana lahyau || suni ke mānasarovara rīti | śraddhā bhaī karī kachu prīti || taba prabodha ke mana kachu āī | raina sarovara base ju jāī || vaisākhī pūnyau kauṁ gayau | mana ekatra kiyau sukha layau || godhana dekhi parama sukha pāyau | pāchaiṁ ṭhaura udāsa janāyau || gharī doya rāti jaba gaī | rītī bhūmi bhayānaka bhaī || pāchaiṁ siṁha-siṁhanī dhāye | tinakī garajana sunata saṁkāye || pāchaiṁ nāga-nāginī dekhe | ḍaryau na viṣadhara bhayada alekhe || pāchaiṁ pavana buhārī daī | bādara ulahyau barasā bhaī || śītala manda sugandha samīra | ānanda bāḍhyau sakala śarīra || prabodhānanda kauṁ nidrā āī | susupta magana tana-daśā bhulāī || kuñjavihārī yahai vicārī | yaha hyāṁ kau nāhīṁ adhikārī || abahīṁ yāke bahut kacāī | rasika saṅga binu bharama na jāī || mathurā kuṭī māñjha pahuñcāyau | mānasarovara rahana na pāyau || prāta jagyau taba mana meṁ āī | nitya-vihāra sahī sukhadāī || paramānanda vacana sata jānyau | apanau haṭha saba jhūṭhau mānyau || taba paramānanda ke ghara āye | saravara ke viratānta sunāye || tumharau vacana bhayau paramāna | nita-vihāra rasa kau kari dāna || taba paramānanda ke mana bhāye | yā rasa ke dātā ju batāye || śrī harivaṁśa caraṇa jaba sevai | taba yā rasa ke jānai bhevai || suni prabodha vṛndāvana āye | darasana kiyed parama sukha pāye || paramānanda prabodha hita kahī | so vinatī hitajū mana gahī || ye sannyāsī hama haiṁ gehī | mana kari bhāva dharau ju sanehī || sevana kari paratīti baḍhāī | nita-vihāra kī śikṣā pāī || stuti aṣṭaka kari suṭhi karī | citta-vṛtti hita-caranani dharī || suni karuṇā kari rīti batāī | abhilāṣā pujaī mana bhāī || nita-vihāra ānanda sunāyau | sukha-sāgara nainani darasāyau || dīpaka sauṁ lagi dīpaka hoī | ekahi dharama na saṁsaya koī || sāvadhāna hvai dhyāna lagāyau | śrī vṛndāvana śata darasāyau || dampati sukha sampati cita lāyau | śrī guru-iṣṭa-sādhu mana bhāyau || rasika ananya dharma paripāṭī | jāni gahī hitajī kī ghāṭī || śrī rādhāvallabha kī kari āsa | sudṛḍha bhayau vṛndāvana vāsa || nita-vihāra rasa varṇana kiyau | rasika janani kau sīñcyau hiyau || nipaṭa rahasya keli kala gāī | vṛndāvana niṣṭhā sudṛḍhāī || kuñja-rahasya grantha bahu kīne | arthani jānati rasika pravīne || śrī prabodhānanda kī, bānī veda pramāna | rasika ananyani kauṁ sukhada, 'bhagavata mudita' sujāna ||

"Prabodhānanda caught Hita Harivaṁśa's feet, and after hearing from him, he gave up the bliss of the impersonal Brahman and attained the happiness of enjoying the eternal pastimes (*nitya-vihāra*)[9] of Rādhā and Kṛṣṇa.

9. *Nitya-vihāra* is a prominent concept in the Rādhā-vallabha-sampradāya, according to which Rādhā and Kṛṣṇa are continuously enjoying amorous pastimes in union, without any scope for separation (*viraha*).

Prabodhānanda was a mendicant *sannyāsī* belonging to a line that followed an impersonalist philosophy. He was just like a second Sarasvatī and conquered all directions with his knowledge. Because he was very learned, he became very arrogant. He came from Kāśī to Vṛndāvana, where he spent one month and obtained great happiness. He visited all temples and met all local *ācāryas*. He became well acquainted with everyone's philosophy, but Prabodha's mind did not accept any of them. Somewhere he met a *rasika* devotee called Paramānanda,[10] and while discussing with each other, both of them became very pleased at heart. They had a discussion about *nitya-vihāra*, but Prabodha was not convinced. Paramānanda presented many evidences from the *śruti, smṛti, itihāsas, āgamas, Sanaka-saṁhitā* and *Vāmana Mahāpurāṇa.* He also mentioned that *rasika* devotees realized *nitya-vihāra* in the Mānasarovara. Hearing about the Mānasarovasa method, Prabodha developed some faith and appreciation for that concept. Then something entered Prabodha's heart. Going to the lake during the full moon of the month Vaiśākha (April-May), he spent the night there with a concentrated mind and felt joy. He became very happy after seeing Govardhana. However, later he felt dejected for not attaining his purpose. Around midnight, the place was desolate and became scary. Then lions started running around, and hearing their roars, he became frightened. He then saw poisonous snakes, but they failed to scare him. The wind began blowing and clouds showered. A gentle, fresh and aromatic breeze filled his

10. He was a disciple of Hita Harivaṁśa.

whole body with joy. Prabodhānanda then fell asleep, and while absorbed in deep sleep, he forgot all bodily discomfort. Lord Kṛṣṇa, Who enjoys pastimes in the groves of Vraja, thought, 'He is not qualified to be in this place. He is still very much inept. Without the association of *rasika* devotees, his confusion cannot be dispelled. He may have reached a hut in Mathurā but has not attained a residence at the Mānasarovara.' When Prabodha woke up in the morning, his mind was convinced that the concept of *nitya-vihāra* actually gives one transcendental bliss. He understood that Paramānanda's words were true and therefore he accepted that his obstinacy was totally wrong. He then went to Paramānanda's house and told him about the incidents at the Mānasarovara. 'Your words proved correct. Kindly impart to me the taste of *nitya-vihāra*. Paramānanda became very pleased at heart and then told him who can give this taste, 'When you serve the feet of Śrī Hita Harivaṁśa, then you will understand the mysteries of *nitya-vihāra rasa.'* Hearing this, Prabodha went to Vṛndāvana and upon having Harivaṁśa's *darśana*, he became very happy. Paramānanda had spoken well of Prabodha to Harivaṁśa, and the latter was captivated by his modesty. He thought, 'He is a *sannyāsī* and I am a householder, yet he is so affectionate that my mind is captivated.' Prabodha served him and their affection grew. He was then taught about *nitya-vihāra*. He composed eight beautiful verses glorifying Harivaṁśa and fixed his mind on his feet. When he heard those verses, Harivaṁśa showed his mercy to him and imparted to him knowledge about the mode of worship in *nitya-vihāra,* thus fulfilling his heart's desire. He told him about the bliss of *nitya-vihāra* and showed that ocean of happiness before his eyes. It was just like a candle lighting another candle. In this way Prabodha had no more doubts about that mode of worship. He started to carefully practice meditation and wrote a collection of verses entitled *'Vṛndāvana-śatakam.'* His heart was always absorbed in the treasure-like happiness of the Divine Couple, and his mind found pleasure in his guru, worshipable deities and saintly persons. He thus understood the exclusive mode of worship performed by *rasika* devotees as taught by Harivaṁśa. Aspiring for Śrī Rādhā-Vallabha, he decided to live in Vṛndāvana permanently. He described the *nitya-vihāra rasa* and thus showered mercy on the *rasika* devotees. He continuously sang the Lord's secret amorous pastimes and was staunchly devoted to Vṛndāvana. He composed many books on the mysteries of the pastimes in the groves of Vṛndāvana, which are known only to the expert *rasika* devotees. The wise Bhagavat Mudita says that Prabodhānanda's words are just like Vedic evidence and give great happiness to the surrendered *rasika* devotees."

Kiśorīśaraṇa Ali gives Saṁvat 1594 (1538 AD)[11] as the year when Prabodha came to Vṛndāvana as an impersonalist *sannyāsī* and was converted by Harivaṁśa. This was four years after the disappearance of Lord Caitanya, so it is not possible that this could be the same person who wrote the *Caitanya-candrāmṛta* and who was the guru of Gopāla Bhaṭṭa Gosvāmī.

11. *Hindī Bhakti Kāvya meṁ Rasa-bhakti Dhārā aur uska Vāṇī Sāhitya*, Vṛndāvana, 1998.

In the *Bhakta-nāmāvalī*, verse 29, Dhruvadāsa (16th – 17th century AD), who is said to be a disciple of Hita Harivaṁśa, states:

> *jugala prema rasa abdhi meṁ paryau prabodha mana jāi |*
> *vṛndāvana rasa mādhurī gāī adhika laḍāi ||*

"Prabodha's mind was always absorbed in the ocean of the transcendental loving mellows of the Divine Couple. With great affection, he sang the sweetness of the *rasas* of Vṛndāvana."

On the basis of these and many more verses written by other authors coming down in the line of Hita Harivaṁśa in the 17th , 18th and 19th centuries, in the appendix of his edition of the *Rādhā-sudhā-nidhi,* Kiśorīśaraṇa Ali makes an extensive analysis of the available information on both Prabodhānandas and summarizes the distinctions of the Rādhā-vallabhī Prabodhānanda as follows:

1. He was a disciple of Śrī Hita Harivaṁśa and even before surrendering to him, without any doubt his name was Prabodhānanda;
2. Before meeting Śrī Hita, he was certainly a monist *sannyāsī*;
3. He definitely came from Kāśī to Vṛndāvana and was originally from Bengal;
4. On the basis of ancient evidences, he arrived in Vṛndāvana between 1538 and 1539 AD;
5. After surrendering to Śrī Hita, he spent the rest of his life within the boundaries of Śrī Vṛndāvana;

6. He definitely surrendered to Śrī Hita in Vṛndāvana;
7. He was exclusively devoted to Śrī Vṛndāvana, the personal abode of Śrī Vṛndāvaneśvarī;
8. He rejects one who leaves Vṛndāvana, one who incites to leave Vṛndāvana, and even a guru who creates hindrances to continuous residence there; not only this, he turns his face away even from Lord Hari Himself if He happens to be outside of Vṛndāvana;
9. He is the author of *Vṛndāvana-śatakam,* which propagates the glories of Śrī Vṛndāvana Dhāma;
10. Abiding by the order of his Gurudeva, he remained in the *sannyāsī* dress;
11. He was a *rasika* exclusively devoted to the *rasa* of Vṛndāvana;
12. He considered the earthly manifestation of Śrī Vṛndāvana as the ultimate goal, superior even to Goloka;
13. He was absorbed in the mood of the Sakhīs and exclusively chanted the mantra consisting in the name of Śrī Rādhā;
14. He meditated on his Gurudeva in the form of a Sakhī servant of Śrī Rādhā and followed in his footsteps.

The above evidence and analysis seem to confirm that there were indeed two Prabodhānandas: the Gauḍīya one, guru of Gopāla Bhaṭṭa Gosvāmī, and the Rādhā-vallabhī one, disciple of Hita Harivaṁśa. The latter is well-known as the author of the *Hita-harivaṁśa-candrāṣṭakam,* the eight verses in praise of Hita Harivaṁśa, which can be seen engraved on the inner walls of the Sevākuñja in Vṛndāvana. This also solves the controversy pertaining to the supposed relationship between Harivaṁśa and the Gauḍīya Prabodhānanda, which was probably no more than another confusion.

Another controversy spread by the Bengali *Bhakta-māla* (20.133) and the *Prema-vilāsa* (18th chapter) attributed to Nityānanda Dāsa, a disciple of Jāhnavā Devī, is the claim that Hita Harivaṁśa was a disciple of Gopāla Bhaṭṭa. Both texts narrate that once the latter saw Harivaṁśa chewing betel *prasāda* on an *ekādaśī* day, scolded him and requested him to abide by the scriptural injunctions. When the same incident happened again, Gopāla Bhaṭṭa asked why he was violating the regulative principles, to which Harivaṁśa admitted to offending him for not following his order, but he could not refuse Śrī Rādhā's *prasāda*. *Prema-vilāsa* goes so far as to say that Harivaṁśa was then deprived of the service to Śrī Rādhā-Ramaṇa and thus installed his own deity, Śrī Rādhā-Vallabha, Whom he worshipped until one day when some dacoits chopped off his head and threw it in the Yamunā. Gopāla Bhaṭṭa was bathing in the Yamunā at that time and was shocked to see the decapitated head shedding tears and crying "Rādhe, Rādhe!" Harivaṁśa's head then floated close to Gopāla Bhaṭṭa and asked for forgiveness. He then took pity on him and put his foot on Harivaṁśa's head, who then attained liberation.

We have already seen above how the Bengali *Bhakta-māla* is not considered a reliable text. This fantastic and ludicrous narration almost precludes the need to pass any comment on the so-called *Prema-vilāsa.* B. B. Majumdar, in the *Caitanya Cariter Upadān* (14th chapter), makes a detailed assessment of the authenticity of the *Prema-vilāsa,* and on the basis of the oldest manuscripts and their contents, he concludes that the text written by Nityānanda Dāsa originally consisted of only sixteen chapters, each of which was largely interpolated in course of time, besides which there was an addition of another eight chapters or more at the end. Each manuscript seems to have a different number of verses in each chapter, and the beginning and end of the chapters also do not match. Many of the narrations are based on dreams and "voices in the sky," supposedly seen and heard by different devotees and include many statements unheard of, such as Lord Nityānanda receiving *dīkṣā* from Īśvara Purī.[12] The book was first printed by Rāma Nārāyaṇa Vidyāratna in the early 1900s with only eighteen chapters. In 1911 AD, he published a second edition with twenty chapters. Yaśodānandana Tālukadāra printed another edition in 1913 AD with twenty-six "and a half" chapters. In the beginning of the text, the author declares that he received an order from Jāhnavā Devī to write down the exploits of Śrīnivāsācārya, Narottama Dāsa Ṭhākura and Śyāmānanda Prabhu, which is the central theme of the entire book up to the sixteenth chapter, after which the topics stray quite far from the original narrative, as we may observe from the supposed incident mentioned above.

12. Vide the 7th chapter.

Hita Harivaṁśa was a prominent religious leader in Vṛndāvana in the 16th century. He had many disciples and established the Śrī Rādhā-Vallabha temple, one of the main temples of Vṛndāvana along with those of Govinda, Madana-mohana and Gopīnātha. It is one of the most visited temples up to the present day. If he had indeed been murdered, there would certainly be clear records documenting this. Particularly we would expect that at least the Gauḍīyas would be eager to show the world the destination of those who offend their gurus. It is more than suspicious that the first time this tale appeared was several centuries later within a text which the Gauḍīyas themselves repudiate as spurious.

In the *Bhramocchedana*,[13] while addressing this guru-disciple controversy, Gopāla Prasāda Śarmā describes an odd incident. According to him, Rādhā-caraṇa Gosvāmī Vidyāvāgīśa, a respectable scholar of the Rādhā-Ramaṇa *parivāra* and former mayor of Vṛndāvana, had mentioned in a book called *Caitanya-carita-sāra* that Hita Harivaṁśa was a disciple of Gopāla Bhaṭṭa Gosvāmī. The indignant Rādhā-vallabhīs then strongly protested and the case was taken to the local police. On the 5th October, 1888, Vidyāvāgīśa supposedly admitted that he had no evidence to support his claim and thus had to pay a five-rupee fine and apologize publicly. It is said that a notice was then printed and distributed all over Vṛndāvana. Although the tone of the narration sounds legitimate, and although

13. A Hindi book published by Mūlacanda Lāla Gosvāmī in Kolkata, 1920, pages 43-50.

it was even quoted by scholars like Dr. Vijayendra Snātaka,[14] I could not find a single trace to corroborate it, despite enquiring far and wide in Vṛndāvana and despite Snātaka's claim that the said printed notice is still preserved. I approached many of the senior and learned Rādhā-vallabhīs in Vṛndāvana, but they could not present a copy of that notice, nor did they seem to be aware of the incident. Furthermore, Vidyāvāgīśa's descendants had never heard of it either. In a biographical thesis[15] on Vidyāvāgīśa written by Dr. Kedāradatta Tatrāḍī, there is not a single word about it. Moreover, there is no work entitled *Caitanya-carita-sāra* among the innumerable publications written by Vidyāvāgīśa, nor a single copy of this book in his personal library. In the absence of any corroborating evidence, we may suspect this to be yet another attempt to taint another's reputation.

Some fertile brains speculate that after being rejected by Gopāla Bhaṭṭa Gosvāmī, Hita Harivaṁśa took shelter of Prabodhānanda Sarasvatī, and for this reason the latter was repudiated by the Gauḍīya community, who shunned his name, which explains why it is not found in the *Caitanya-caritāmṛta*. In the *Bhakti-ratnākara,* Narahari Cakravartī has been kind enough to demystify the silence of Kavirāja Gosvāmī:

---

14. *Rādhā-vallabha Sampradāya: Siddhānta aur Sāhitya*, New Delhi, 1958, third chapter, page 104.

15. *Śrī Gosvāmī Rādhā-caraṇa jī: Vyaktitva tathā kṛtitva*, Vṛndāvana, 1995

śrī-gopāla-bhaṭṭa hṛṣṭa haiyā ājñā dila |
granthe nija-prasaṅga varṇite niṣedhila || 1.222 ||

kene niṣedhila, ihā ke bujhite pāre |
nirantara atidīna māne āpanāre || 1.223 ||

kavirāja tāṁra ājñā nāre laṅghibāre |
nāma-mātra likhe anya na kare pracāre || 1.224 ||

"Śrīla Gopāla Bhaṭṭa was also pleased to give Kṛṣṇadāsa an order to write the book but forbade Kṛṣṇadāsa to write about him (Gopāla Bhaṭṭa). Who can understand why he forbade him? He always considered himself very low. Śrīla Kavirāja Gosvāmī would not violate his order, therefore he only mentioned his name without describing his glories."

Out of humility, Gopāla Bhaṭṭa and Prabodhānanda insisted that they should not be glorified in the *Caitanya-caritāmṛta.* This explanation is quite plausible, and since Narahari was coming from the spiritual lineage of Gopāla Bhaṭṭa, it is probable that this is the version he heard from his predecessors. If the above claim is true and Prabodhānanda was therefore not glorified by Kavirāja Gosvāmī, then for what reason was Gopāla Bhaṭṭa not glorified either? His name was merely mentioned six times in the *Caitanya-caritāmṛta* in unavoidable contexts, such as when naming the six Gosvāmīs of Vṛndāvana, but he was not the subject of any narration in the whole book, despite the fact that each of the other five Gosvāmīs had their life stories outlined. Moreover, if Prakāśānanda and

Prabodhānanda were the same person, Kavirāja Gosvāmī would have violated his request not to write about him, and the highlight on his life in Vārāṇasī would be totally inconsistent due to the omission about his previous and later life in Śrīraṅgam and Vṛndāvana. Otherwise we may wonder how it is possible that those in the line of Gopāla Bhaṭṭa were unaware of such an important fact about his guru Prabodhānanda. And also, why Narahari would speak such nonsense? By not informing the readers that Prakāśānanda later became Prabodhānanda, Kavirāja's narration would be faulty and he would be accountable for hundreds of years of confusion.

Prabodhānanda Sarasvatī was an incarnation of Tuṅgavidyā, was born in a pure Śrī Vaiṣṇava family, became the guru of Gopāla Bhaṭṭa and attained the personal association of Lord Caitanya. Although he did not have the slightest blemish, the Gauḍīyas themselves mercilessly turned him into a *māyāvādī* leper called Prakāśānanda and continue to depict him as such without hesitation or embarrassment. If they can be so ruthless to Prabodhānanda, what would they not speak about Śrī Hita Harivaṁśa, given that the animosity between the Rādhā-vallabhīs and the Gauḍīyas began from their very primordial days and continues up to the present? In the absence of strong and unambiguous evidence, the myth that Prabodhānanda was Prakāśānanda is no less a hoax than the myth that Harivaṁśa was a rejected disciple of Gopāla Bhaṭṭa Gosvāmī.

There are yet two other controversies regarding Prabodhānanda Sarasvatī. A rumour says that he worshipped Lord Caitanya in the mood of the Gaurāṅga-nāgarīs,[16] which seems to have been originated from his use of the expression 'gaura-nāgara' in the *Caitanya-candrāmṛta* (132). Vṛndāvanadāsa Ṭhākura rebuked such expression in the *Caitanya-bhāgavata*, 1.15.30:

ataeva yata mahā-mahima sakale 'gaurāṅga-nāgara' hena stava nāhi bale

"Therefore, great personalities do not praise Lord Caitanya by calling him 'Gaurāṅga-nāgara,' the lover of damsels."

For this reason, some assume that Prabodhānanda was excommunicated by the Gauḍīyas, who therefore avoided his name and works. This is another highly speculative slander that contradicts the respect offered to Prabodhānanda by stalwart *ācāryas* like Gopāla Bhaṭṭa, Jīva Gosvāmī and Sanātana Gosvāmī. As mentioned above, the *Bhakti-ratnākara* explains the factual reason why his name was not often mentioned. First of all, there is no evidence that Vṛndāvana dāsa was speaking about Prabodhānanda Sarasvatī. Secondly, the meanings of the word 'nāgara' in Sanskrit and vernacular are different. While in Bengali this word is primarily used in the sense of 'lover' and 'paramour,' in Sanskrit it is not. In his Bengali translation to

16. "The girlfriends of Gaurāṅga," an *apasampradāya* in which the worshippers consider themselves *gopīs* and see Caitanya Mahāprabhu as Kṛṣṇa in Vṛndāvana in the form of a paramour (nāgara) enjoyer of the *gopīs*.

the said verse, Śrīla Bhaktisiddhānta Sarasvatī explains that the word 'nāgara' means 'parama-rasika,' transcendental enjoyer of *rasa*. It particularly depicts Kṛṣṇa, Who has now appeared in a golden (gaura) form.[17]

There is also an old dispute over the authorship of the *Rādhā-rasa-sudhā-nidhi, Vṛndāvana-mahimāmṛta* and *Saṅgīta-Mādhava,* which the Rādhā-vallabhīs claim to have been written by their *ācāryas.* Recently they have filed a judicial case against the Gauḍīyas who claim that the *Rādhā-rasa-sudhā-nidhi* was authored by the Gauḍīya Prabodhānanda Sarasvatī instead of Hita Harivaṁśa, whom they believe to be the real author. This problem will be solved only when all extant ancient manuscripts are collected and properly analysed.

Viveka-śatakam

The first known mention of this work was by Rājendra Lāla Mitra[18] in 1883. He gave the following description to the manuscript number 2510:

Substance: country-made paper, 13 X 4 inches. Folio: 6. Lines: 13 on a page. Extent: 100 ślokas. Character: Bengali. Date: ? Place of deposit: Bahrāmpur, Bābu Rāmadāsa Sen. Appearance: old. Verse: Correct. A century of verses on dispassion or indifference

17. For more on this topic, vide Bhaktisidhānta Sarasvatī Ṭhākura's commentaries on the *Caitanya-bhāgavata,* Ādi-khaṇḍa 15.17-32, and the Bengali magazine *Gauḍīya*, second year, volume II, pages 6-9.

18. *Notices of Sanskrit Manuscripts*, Volume VII, part I, Kolkata, 1883.

to worldly attractions for the sake of devotion to Kṛṣṇa, by Prabodhānanda Sarasvatī.

After that, for many decades the whereabouts of this manuscript was unknown and therefore it remained unpublished until now. At this point it is difficult to ascertain their trajectory, but somehow many of the manuscripts that belonged to Bābu Rāmadāsa Sen are now preserved at the National Library of India, Kolkata, including the *Viveka-śatakam*. Although no date is mentioned, based on the paper, ink and style, we may infer that it was probably written in the first half of the 17th century AD, or perhaps even earlier. There are indications that it was a transcription from an original in Devanāgarī, and despite Mitra's description, there is indeed a good amount of incorrectness.

Besides that, only one more manuscript copy has been located so far, belonging to the Khasmohor collection, accession number 6040, Mahārāja Mān Singh II Museum in Jaipur. This collection belonged to King Sawai Jai Singh II (1688-1743 AD), and contains many manuscripts that were copied and composed under his order. The characteristics of this manuscript indicate that it was probably written at the beginning of the 18th century AD, but no date is stated. Although the script is Devanāgarī and the handwriting is quite intelligible, in this case also the scribe made many errors, fortunately usually not in the same places as in the Bengali manuscript. Thus, both manuscripts were complementary and essential to have an accurate picture of the original text. Since Prabodhānanda wrote this work while he was still a householder living in Tamil Naḍu, it is possible that the original might have been written in Tamil script, as commonly done in those days. Once in Vṛndāvana, it was desirable that his writings should be available in Devanāgarī, therefore someone possibly made a transcription of the *Viveka-śatakam* in which some words and characters may have been incorrectly written. This first transcription in Devanāgarī could have been the basis for other copies and transcriptions, such as in Bengali script, which would naturally contain further mistakes.

The text sheds enough light on Prabodhānanda's life and definitely dismisses any possibility that he was ever a *māyāvādī sannyāsī*. In verses 1, 6 and 38, the author states that he is already in old age and his body is collapsing due to decrepitude. From this we can conclude that he was not less than sixty years old when he wrote this, possibly much older. In verses 4, 6, 7, 47, 70, 79, 81, and 91, he directly and indirectly speaks about his experience and impressions about kings and rich men. Several times he reveals that he served kings to support himself and his family, although he does not tell us exactly in which capacity. In verses 5, 21, 45, 46, 52, 67, 68, and 69, the author shares his realizations about family life, its anxieties and frustrations. Throughout the book, he repeatedly expresses his wish to go to Vṛndāvana. In verse 9, he directly states that he wants to leave his present residence, and in verses 1 and 6, he laments for being so far away from Vṛndāvana. Since there is no hint that he was living in a holy place, perhaps in those days Prabodhānanda was no more living in Śrīraṅgam but somewhere else in Tamil Naḍu, which at any rate is actually very far from Vṛndāvana. From verse 21 it seems that he also had experience in business, but from verse 19 it is clear that he was born in a *brāhmaṇa* family. In verse 81, he mentions that marking the body with sandalwood paste in the form of conch, disc, etc. is the only ornament of devotees. This is a traditional practice peculiar to South Indian Vaiṣṇavas and is another evidence that the author was indeed from the South. Although Lord Caitanya's name is not directly mentioned anywhere in the text, Prabodhānanda's adherence to His philosophy is understood from many verses. In verses 64, 75, 76, 78, and 95, he expresses his desire to serve the Lord birth after birth. In verse 13, he declares that Kṛṣṇa, the Lord of Gokula, is superior even to Lord Viṣṇu. Śrīmatī Rādhārāṇī's name appears in verses 73, 74, 75, and 78, and the name Rādhā-ramaṇa appears in verses 43 and 45, which hints that this name had a special significance to him. All this is consistent with what we hear from the *Bhakti-ratnākara* and the conclusions presented by Śrīla Bhaktisiddhānta Sarasvatī.

In this work, the author used eight different varieties of metres as follows:

Mālabhāriṇī (11 and 12 syllables): 22

Madhumādhavī (14 syllables): 11, 26, 28

Mālinī (15 syllables): 16, 67, 68, 69, 93

Pṛthvī (17 syllables): 8, 14, 25, 49, 83, 94

Mandākrāntā (17 syllables): 1, 27, 29, 43, 48, 61, 85, 86

Śikhariṇī (17 syllables): 2, 3, 12, 13, 19, 20, 32, 33, 34, 35, 36, 40, 45, 46, 47, 50, 52, 55, 56, 57, 60, 62, 63, 64, 65, 70, 82, 84

Śārdūlavikrīḍita (19 syllables): 4, 5, 6, 7, 9, 10, 15, 18, 23, 30, 31, 37, 38, 39, 42, 54, 58, 59, 66, 71, 72, 73, 76, 77, 78, 79, 80, 81, 87, 88, 89, 90, 91, 92, 95, 96, 97, 98, 99, 100

Śragdharā (21 syllables): 17, 21, 24, 41, 44, 51, 53, 74, 75

Caitanya-citrāṣṭakam

This work was mentioned by Haridāsa Dāsa in the *Gauḍīya Vaiṣṇava Abhidhāna*, and up to the present day, there are three manuscript copies preserved at the Gaurāṅga Grantha Mandira in Kolkata:

Gaurāṅga-sudhākara-citrāṣṭakam, acc. number 1380/41
Gaura-sudhākara-citrāṣṭakam, acc. number 1447/74
Caitanya-citrāṣṭakam, acc. number 1392/46

While analysing the manuscripts, it becomes apparent why this text has not been published – the first one is badly damaged, and all three of them have faulty readings written by scribes who were obviously clueless about Sanskrit. None of the manuscripts are dated, but the first two copies seem to be more than three centuries old, and the third may be a couple of centuries old. All of them are in Bengali script and have both common mistakes as well as unique mistakes. By a meticulous cross-study it was possible to correct the readings according to grammar, prosody and the logical contextual meaning. We do not know whether this composition preceded *Caitanya-candrāmṛta* or not, but some of the motifs and similes utilized by Prabodhānanda appear in both. The metre is Śārdūlavikrīḍita, which was the most frequent metre used in the *Viveka-śatakam.*

Nityānandāṣṭakam

These verses were published for the first time in Kolkata in 1880 AD in a compilation entitled *Vaiṣṇavācāra-darpaṇa* by Navadvīpa Candra Gosvāmī, who attributed their authorship to Vṛndāvana dāsa Ṭhākura. In 1894 AD, the same *Nityānandāṣṭakam* was published in Agartala by Kṛṣṇa Candra Varma, who attributed it to Kṛṣṇadāsa Kavirāja. In 1901 AD, in a new edition of the *Vaiṣṇavācāra-darpaṇa,* Navadvīpa Candra Gosvāmī added an extensive note in which he accuses Varma of intentionally using Kṛṣṇa Kavirāja's name to promote Lord Nityānanda's worship. He points out that the readers have naturally become confused after seeing this disagreement over the authorship and tries to solve it by criticizing Varma's interpretations of the verses and establishing Vṛndāvana dāsa Ṭhākura's authorship on the basis of his statements on the *Caitanya-bhāgavata,* etc. Curiously enough, neither of these publishers bothered to search for ancient manuscripts in order to present legitimate evidence rather than mere assumptions. Needless to say, they were obviously dealing with an unnamed copy of the text. It is quite common that short poetical compositions of different authors were copied together in a single volume, and often their names would not be mentioned at the end as we may expect. This naturally led to speculations and misunderstandings, and in many instances, texts ended up being published in the name of someone else rather than the real author's. Although Navadvīpa Candra's effort seems to have prevailed and this *Nityānandāṣṭakam* was afterwards published many times in the name of Vṛndāvana dāsa, since he failed to present a named manuscript, his claims are as meaningful as Varma's. Despite extensive search, I could not locate a single manuscript copy of this text in which the name of Vṛndāvana dāsa Ṭhākura is mentioned. He does have a *Nityānandāṣṭakam* to his credit, but it is different than the one published by the above-mentioned gentlemen. Moreover, there are still incorrect readings in the available editions of the Sanskrit text and the translations contain wrong interpretations.

The discovery of a manuscript in whose colophon the name of Prabodhānanda Sarasvatī is clearly mentioned as the author is quite opportune to solve this old controversy for good. Though I deliberately searched for the *Viveka-śatakam* and *Caitanya-citrāṣṭakam*, the *Nityānandāṣṭakam* was unexpectedly placed in my hands just when I was about to publish those two texts. Once I came to know that Śrī Rādhā-caraṇa Gosvāmī Vidyāvāgīśa's personal library in Vṛndāvana had been closed and unattended for many decades. I then contacted his descendent, Śrī Caitanya Gosvāmī, and after some deliberation, at my request he donated the whole collection of printed books and manuscripts to the Jīva Institute, where they are still in the process of renovation and classification. Recently Dr. Jayesh Khandewal, director of the Rasa Bhāratī Institute and owner of the Khandewal Book Shop in Vṛndāvana, contacted me to have a look at the said collection. While perusing the manuscripts, he expressed curiosity about a particular one which he could not read because it was written in Bengali script. When he handed it to me to satisfy his doubt, I experienced both surprise and joy to see the sentence *iti śrī-prabodhānanda-sarasvatī-viracitaṁ nityānandāṣṭakaṁ samāptam,* "Thus ends the *Nityānandāṣṭakam* composed by Śrī Prabodhānanda Sarasvatī." Yet since there is no date, this could considerably make its authenticity doubtful. I therefore consulted Paṇḍita Vrindavan Bihari Goswami, a reputed manuscriptogy scholar who worked as a classifier in the Vrindavan Research Institute for three decades, as well as Paṇḍita Tilak Sharma, owner of the Sanjay Museum in Jaipur, which hosts the largest private collection of manuscripts in the world. They examined the manuscript and both of them agreed that all its characteristics indicate that it belongs to the late 16th century AD. This rules out the chance that it was deliberately written in Prabodhānanda's name, who was far from being a renowned author in those days. A Devanāgarī manuscript, preserved at the Government Oriental Manuscript Library in Chennai, R.3053 (b), was also helpful to correct wrong readings.

As it was the case in the *Caitanya-citrāṣṭakam,* here too the author utilizes themes and similes that appear in other of his works.

Verse 1: "A face more beautiful than the autumn moon," and "elephant-like gait" are also seen in the *Caitanya-candrāmṛta.*[19] "Eyes rolling in ecstasy" also appears in the *Vṛndāvana-mahimāmṛta.*[20]

Verse 2: "Unknown to the fools" is also seen in the *Vṛndāvana-mahimāmṛta.*[21]

Verse 3: "Bliss personified" is also seen in the *Vṛndāvana-mahimāmṛta.*[22]

Verse 4: "Atonement for sinful activities" is also seen in the *Vṛndāvana-mahimāmṛta.* [23]

Verse 5: "Saviour of the souls contaminated by Kali" is also seen in the *Viveka-śatakam,* 22; "Chanting 'Hari, Hari' with raised arms" and "chanting to cross the ocean of material existence" also appears in the *Caitanya-candrāmṛta* .[24]

---

19. *śrīman-mukhendu-cchaṭā-vicchāyīkṛta-koṭi-koṭi-śarad-unmīlat-tuṣāra-cchaviḥ* (74 or 92); *gati-jita-pronmatta-koṭi-dvipaḥ* (103 or 140).

20. *madāghūrṇad-ākarṇa-netrā* (14.87)

21. *govinda-pādāmbuja-dvandve manda-dhiyo vidanti na hi* (1.51)

22. *na punaḥ paratra sac-cit-sukha-mayam api durlabhaṁ devaiḥ* (3.53); *tad vṛndāvanam adbhutaṁ sukha-mayaṁ ko nāma nālambate* (17.68).

23. *prāyaścittam aghāni* (4.88).

24. *bāhū proddhṛtya sat-tāṇḍava-tarala-tanuṁ puṇḍarīkāyatākṣam | viśvasyāmaṅgalaghnaṁ kim api hari-harīty unmadānanda-nādaiḥ*

Verse 6: "Merciful side-glances" also appears in the *Caitanya-candrāmṛta.*[25]

Verse 7: "Like a second Agastya Muni" also appears in the *Viveka-śatakam,* 28.

Verse 8: The interjection 'ahaha' appears nine times among the 143 verses of *Caitanya-candrāmṛta,* 55 times among the 1769 verses of *Vṛndāvana-mahimāmṛta,* and twice among the hundred verses of *Viveka-śatakam.* In contrast, it does not appear even once in the *Śrīmad-Bhāgavatam.*

The metre of the *Nityānandāṣṭakam* is Śikhariṇī, the second most used metre in the *Viveka-śatakam.*

This publication would not have been possible without the help of several individuals and institutions. The respective staffs of the Mahārāja Mān Singh II Museum in Jaipur, the National Library of India in Kolkata, the Gaurāṅga Grantha Mandira in Kolkata, and the Government Oriental Manuscript Library in Chennai assisted me during my repeated visits. Dr. Satyanārāyaṇa dāsa, director of the Jīva Institute, always maintains the doors of his library and ashram open for me. Vikram Majumdar accompanied me in several expeditions in West Bengal. BV Giri Swami, Rameṣṭa dāsa, Jagannivāsa dāsa, Mahāprabhu dāsa, and Dīnanātha dāsa helped editing and revising different portions of the translation

(10 or 65); *saṁsāra-sindhu-taraṇe hṛdayaṁ yadi syāt saṅkīrtanāmṛta-rase* (93 or 143).

25. *caitanya-candra yadi te karuṇā-kaṭākṣaḥ* (55 or 62).

and introduction. Puṣkara dāsa kindly allowed us to have one of his paintings on the cover. Bhīṣmadeva dāsa kindly designed the cover. Bhakti Vikāsa Swami has been continuously supporting the Baladeva Vidyābhūṣaṇa Project and kindly came forward to print this edition. I am very grateful to all of them and all those who also have been directly or indirectly helping this project in any capacity.

Dr. Demian Martins

Śrī Vṛndāvana Dhāma
5th April, 2017, Śrī Rāma navamī

Real Samādhi of Śrīla Prabodhānanda Sarasvatī, Kāliya-ghāṭa, Vṛndāvana

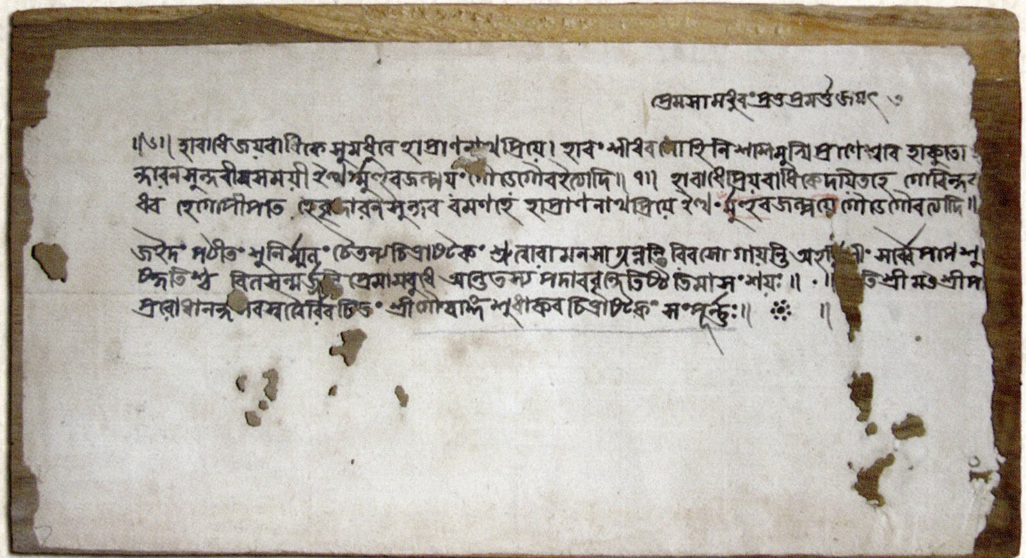

Colophon of a manuscript of the *Caitanya-citrāṣṭakam*, 17th – 18th century AD.

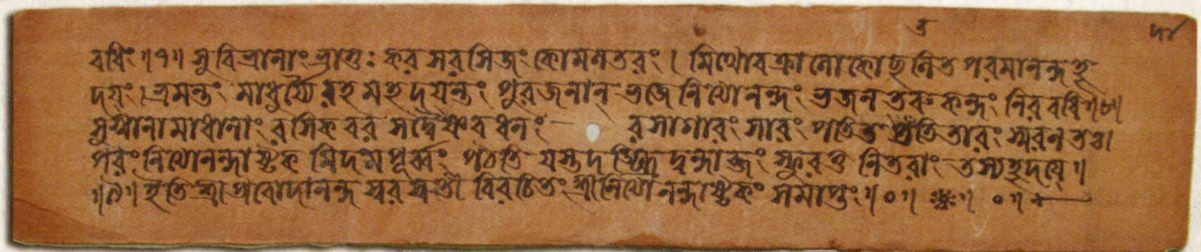

Colophon of a manuscript of the *Nityānandāṣṭakam,* late 16th century AD.

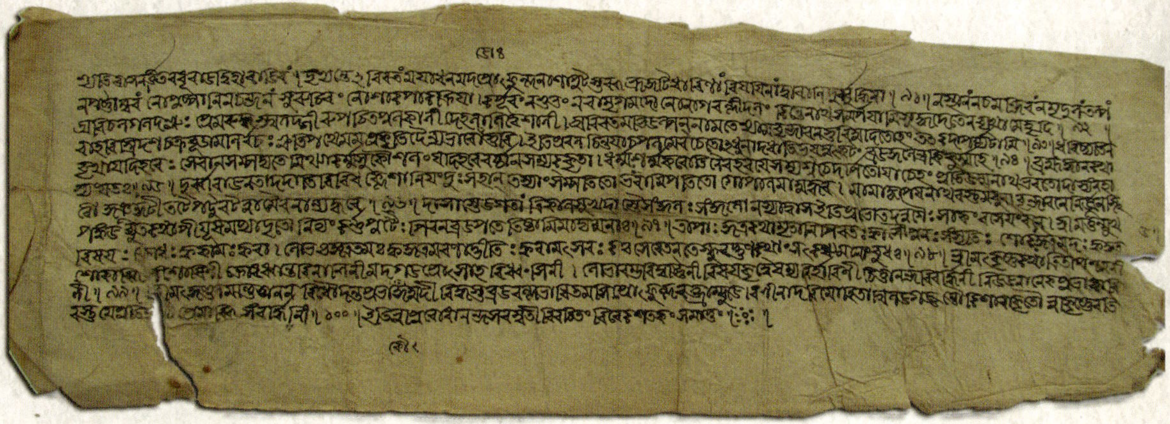

Colophon of a manuscript of the *Viveka-śatakam*, early 17th century AD.

Śrī-Caitanya-citrāṣṭakam

TEXT 1

अन्तर्घोरघनं तमोऽपि निचयं सम्यक्स्वदूरं गतं
पाषण्डो भगवत्परो भवति च त्यक्त्वा स्वकीयं चरम् ।
संतृप्तो भुवनत्रये जनमहास्निग्धोऽपि प्रेमामृतैर्
गौडे गौरसुधाकरे समुदिते किं किं विचित्रं न हि ॥ १ ॥

antar ghora-ghanaṁ tamo 'pi nicayaṁ samyak sva-dūraṁ gataṁ
pāṣaṇḍo bhagavat-paro bhavati ca tyaktvā svakīyaṁ caram |
saṁtṛpto bhuvana-traye jana-mahā-snigdho 'pi premāmṛtair
gauḍe gaura-sudhākare samudite kiṁ kiṁ vicitraṁ na hi || 1 ||

Word-For-Word Meanings

antaḥ – within; *ghora-ghanam* – terrible and dense; *tamaḥ* – darkness; *api* – and; *nicayam* – mass of contamination; *samyak* – completely; *sva-dūram* – far from oneself; *gatam* – gone; *pāṣaṇḍaḥ* – heretic; *bhagavat-paraḥ* – devoted to the Supreme Lord; *bhavati* – becomes; *ca* – and; *tyaktvā* – having given up; *svakīyam* – one's own; *caram* – way of life; *saṁtṛptaḥ* – fully satisfied; *bhuvana-traye* – in the three worlds; *jana-mahā-snigdhaḥ* – very affectionate towards the people; *api* – also; *premāmṛtaiḥ* – with the nectar of love of God; *gauḍe* – in Gauḍadeśa; *gaura-sudhākare* – moon-like Gaurāṅga; *samudite* – having appeared; *kiṁ kiṁ* – what; *vicitram* – wonderful; *na* – not; *hi* – indeed.

Translation

As the moon-like Lord Gaurāṅga appeared in Gauḍadeśa, the terrible darkness and the dense mass of contamination within the heart are now completely gone far from oneself. Having given up his way of life, even a heretic becomes a devotee of the Supreme Lord, and being fully satisfied with the nectar of love of God, he also becomes very affectionate towards all the inhabitants of the three worlds. Is this not wonderful?

TEXT 2

पङ्गुर्लङ्घयते महागिरिवरं बीजं विना चाङ्कुरं
जन्मान्धोऽपि च दिव्यदृष्टिभवितो मूको वदान्यो भवेत् ।
अक्लेशं खलु निर्भरेण सहसा हर्षोऽपि धत्ते स्थिरो
गौडे गौरसुधाकरे समुदिते किं किं विचित्रं न हि ॥ २ ॥

paṅgur laṅghayate mahā-giri-varaṁ bījaṁ vinā cāṅkuraṁ
janmāndho 'pi ca divya-dṛṣṭi-bhavito mūko vadānyo bhavet |
akleśaṁ khalu nirbhareṇa sahasā harṣo 'pi dhatte sthiro
gauḍe gaura-sudhākare samudite kiṁ kiṁ vicitraṁ na hi || 2 ||

Word-For-Word Meanings

paṅguḥ – a lame man; *laṅghayate* – crosses; *mahā-giri-varam* – the best of great mountains; *bījam* – seed; *vinā* – without; *ca* – and; *aṅkuram* – sprout; *janmāndhaḥ* – blind since birth; *api* – even; *ca* – and; *divya-dṛṣṭi-bhavitaḥ* – becomes endowed with divine vision; *mūkaḥ* – dumb; *vadānyaḥ* – eloquent; *bhavet* – would become; *akleśam* – freedom from distress; *khalu* – indeed; *nirbhareṇa* –

without measure; *sahasā* – suddenly; *harṣaḥ* – joy; *api* – also; *dhatte* – produces; *sthiraḥ* – steady; *gauḍe* – in Gauḍadeśa; *gaura-sudhākare* – moon-like Gaurāṅga; *samudite* – having appeared; *kiṁ kim* – what; *vicitram* – wonderful; *na* – not; *hi* – indeed.

Translation

As the moon-like Lord Gaurāṅga appeared in Gauḍadeśa, lame men cross the greatest mountains, sprouts germinate without seeds, and even blind men become endowed with divine vision. Suddenly, steady joy beyond measure produces a feeling of freedom from all distress. Is this not wonderful?

TEXT 3

काचः काञ्चनतां गतोऽपि निखिलं स्वर्णस्तु चिन्तामणिं
वैदूर्योऽतुलरत्नसादृशभवः काकाः खगेन्द्रा इव ।
शाखोटस्तरुरेव चन्दनधरो रण्डश्च कल्पद्रुमो
गौडे गौरसुधाकरे समुदिते किं किं विचित्रं न हि ॥ ३ ॥

kācaḥ kāñcanatāṁ gato 'pi nikhilaṁ svarṇas tu cintāmaṇiṁ
vaidūryo 'tula-ratna-sādṛśa-bhavaḥ kākāḥ khagendrā iva |
śākhoṭas tarur eva candana-dharo raṇḍaś ca kalpa-drumo
gauḍe gaura-sudhākare samudite kiṁ kiṁ vicitraṁ na hi ||3||

Word-For-Word Meanings

kācaḥ – glass; *kāñcanatām* – into gold; *gataḥ* – gone; *api* – also; *nikhilam* – completely; *svarṇaḥ* – gold; *tu* – and; *cintāmaṇim* – philosopher's stone; *vaidūryaḥ* – Vaidūrya gem; *atula-ratna-sādṛśa-bhavaḥ* – producing similar matchless jewels; *kākāḥ* – crows; *khagendrāḥ* – kings of birds; *iva* – like; *śākhoṭaḥ* – Trophis aspera (a small, crooked, ugly tree); *taruḥ* – tree; *eva* – indeed; *candana-dharaḥ* – holding sandalwood; *raṇḍaḥ* – a barren tree; *ca* – and; *kalpa-drumaḥ* – a desire-fulfilling tree; *gauḍe* – in Gauḍadeśa; *gaura-sudhākare* – moon-like Gaurāṅga; *samudite* – having appeared; *kiṁ kim* – what; *vicitram* – wonderful; *na* – not; *hi* – indeed.

Translation

As the moon-like Lord Gaurāṅga appeared in Gauḍadeśa, glass turns into gold; gold becomes the philosopher's stone; Vaidūrya gems produce similar matchless jewels; crows become like Garuḍa; crooked, ugly trees become sandalwood trees; and barren trees become wish-fulfilling trees. Is this not wonderful?

TEXT 4

ब्रह्माद्यैरपि वाञ्छितं मुनिवरैर्भाव्यं च लक्ष्म्यादिकैर्
एवंप्रेम सुदुर्लभं नवसुधा सम्पूर्णभूतं कलौ ।
चाण्डालावधिपापपामरजनाः प्रेमोज्ज्वलं लेभिरे
गौडे गौरसुधाकरे समुदिते किं किं विचित्रं न हि ॥ ४ ॥

brahmādyair api vāñchitaṁ muni-varair bhāvyaṁ ca lakṣmy-ādikair
evaṁ-prema sudurlabhaṁ nava-sudhā sampūrṇa-bhūtaṁ kalau |
cāṇḍālāvadhi-pāpa-pāmara-janāḥ premojjvalaṁ lebhire
gauḍe gaura-sudhākare samudite kiṁ kiṁ vicitraṁ na hi || 4 ||

Word-For-Word Meanings

brahmādyaiḥ – by Lord Brahmā and other demigods; *api* – even; *vāñchitam* – desired; *muni-varaiḥ* – by the best sages; *bhāvyam* – to be apprehended; *ca* – and; *lakṣmy-ādikaiḥ* – by Lakṣmī and others; *evaṁ-prema* – such love for God; *sudurlabham* – very hard to be obtained; *nava-sudhā* – fresh nectar; *sampūrṇa-bhūtam* – attained plenitude; *kalau* – in Kali-yuga; *cāṇḍālāvadhi-pāpa-pāmara-janāḥ* – foolish and sinful people, down to the dog eaters; *prema* – love of God; *ujjvalam* – burning; *lebhire* – obtained; *gauḍe* – in Gauḍadeśa; *gaura-sudhākare* – moon-like Gaurāṅga; *samudite* – having appeared; *kiṁ kim* – what; *vicitram* – wonderful; *na* – not; *hi* – indeed.

Translation

As the moon-like Lord Gaurāṅga appeared in Gauḍadeśa, such love of God, which is like fresh nectar and is very hard to obtain, although desired by the greatest sages such as Lord Brahmā and yet to be comprehended even by Lakṣmī and others, has attained plenitude in this Kali-yuga. Now even foolish and sinful people, down to the dog eaters, have obtained such burning love of God. Is this not wonderful?

TEXT 5

वृन्दारण्यरहस्यकेलिसदने लुप्तातिकालक्रमे
ख्याता चैवमभूत्समस्तसुखदा लीलाकथामाधुरी ।

गोविन्देति व्रजेन्द्रमित्रतनया साक्षाद्रभू राजते
गौडे गौरसुधाकरे समुदिते किं किं विचित्रं न हि ॥ ५ ॥

vṛndāraṇya-rahasya-keli-sadane luptātikāla-krame
khyātā caivam abhūt samasta-sukha-dā līlā-kathā-mādhurī |
govindeti vrajendra-mitra-tanayā sākṣād rabhū rājate
gauḍe gaura-sudhākare samudite kiṁ kiṁ vicitraṁ na hi || 5 ||

Word-For-Word Meanings

vṛndāraṇya-rahasya-keli-sadane – in a secluded place of pastimes in Vṛndāvana; *luptā* – lost; *atikāla-krame* – in a long period of time; *khyātā* – well-known; *ca* – and; *evam* – thus; *abhūt* – became; *samasta-sukha-dā* – which gives complete happiness; *līlā-kathā-mādhurī* – the sweetness of the narrations of the pastimes of the Lord; *govinda* – O Govinda; *iti* – thus; *vrajendra-mitra-tanayā* – the daughter of the friend of the King of Vraja; *sākṣāt* – directly; *rabhū* – messenger; *rājate* – appears; *gauḍe* – in Gauḍadeśa; *gaura-sudhākare* – moon-like Gaurāṅga; *samudite* – having appeared; *kiṁ kim* – what; *vicitram* – wonderful; *na* – not; *hi* – indeed.

Translation

As the moon-like Lord Gaurāṅga appeared in Gauḍadeśa, the sweetness of the narrations of Lord Kṛṣṇa's pastimes, which gives complete happiness, and which in a long period of time was lost in a secluded place of pastimes in Vṛndāvana, has thus become well-known. Exclaiming 'Govinda! Govinda!,' the daughter of Bhānu Mahārāja Herself has now appeared as a messenger. Is this not wonderful?

TEXT 6

राधाकृष्णपदारविन्दभजनानन्दोत्सवाहर्निशं
कृष्णाराधनकृष्णकीर्तनमुदाप्रेमामृतास्वादनम् ।
सर्वे विश्वचराचरप्रभृतयः प्रेमाम्बुधौ मग्नवद्
गौडे गौरसुधाकरे समुदिते किं किं विचित्रं न हि ॥ ६ ॥

rādhā-kṛṣṇa-padāravinda-bhajanānandotsavāhar-niśaṁ
kṛṣṇārādhana-kṛṣṇa-kīrtana-mudā-premāmṛtāsvādanam |
sarve viśva-carācara-prabhṛtayaḥ premāmbudhau magnavad
gauḍe gaura-sudhākare samudite kiṁ kiṁ vicitraṁ na hi || 6 ||

Word-For-Word Meanings

rādhā-kṛṣṇa-padāravinda-bhajanānandotsavāhar-niśam – the festive bliss of serving the lotus feet of Rādhā and Kṛṣṇa day and night; *kṛṣṇārādhana-kṛṣṇa-kīrtana-mudā-premāmṛtāsvādanam* – tasting the nectar of love and the joy of glorifying and worshipping Kṛṣṇa; *sarve* – all; *viśva-carācara-prabhṛtayaḥ* – the moving and non-moving beings in the universe, etc.; *premāmbudhau* – in the ocean of love of God; *magnavat* – as if immersed; *gauḍe* – in Gauḍadeśa; *gaura-sudhākare* – moon-like Gaurāṅga; *samudite* – having appeared; *kiṁ kim* – what; *vicitram* – wonderful; *na* – not; *hi* – indeed.

Translation

As the moon-like Lord Gaurāṅga appeared in Gauḍadeśa, feeling the festive bliss of serving the lotus feet of Rādhā and Kṛṣṇa day and night, and tasting the nectar of love and the joy of glorifying and worshipping Kṛṣṇa, all moving and non-moving beings in the universe became as if immersed in an ocean of love of God. Is this not wonderful?

TEXT 7

हा राधे जय राधिके सुमधुरे हा प्राणनाथप्रिये
हा वंशीधरमोहिनी शशिमुखी प्राणेश्वरी हा कुतः ।
हा वृन्दावनसुन्दरी रसमयीतित्थं मुहुर्जल्पयद्
गौडे गौरसुधाकरे समुदिते किं किं विचित्रं न हि ॥ ७ ॥

hā rādhe jaya rādhike su-madhure hā prāṇa-nātha-priye
hā vaṁśī-dhara-mohinī śaśi-mukhī prāṇeśvarī hā kutaḥ |
hā vṛndāvana-sundarī rasa-mayītitthaṁ muhur jalpayad
gauḍe gaura-sudhākare samudite kiṁ kiṁ vicitraṁ na hi || 7 ||

Word-For-Word Meanings

hā rādhe – ah, Rādhā; *jaya* – all glories; *rādhike* – ah, Rādhikā; *su- madhure* – so sweet; *hā prāṇa-nātha-priye* – ah, beloved of the Lord of my life; *hā* – ah; *vaṁśī-dhara-mohinī* – the enchantress of the flute player; *śaśi-mukhī* – moon-faced; *prāṇeśvarī* – the queen of my life; *hā* – ah; *kutaḥ* – where; *hā* – alas; *vṛndāvana-sundarī* – the beauty of Vṛndāvana; *rasa-mayī* – *rasa* personified; *iti* – thus; *ittham* – in this way; *muhuḥ* – repeatedly; *jalpayat* – murmuring; *gauḍe* – in Gauḍadeśa; *gaura-sudhākare* – moon-like Gaurāṅga; *samudite* – having appeared; *kiṁ kim* – what; *vicitram* – wonderful; *na* – not; *hi* – indeed.

Translation

As the moon-like Lord Gaurāṅga appeared in Gauḍadeśa, the whole world is repeatedly murmuring thus: 'Ah, Rādhā!

All glories unto You. Ah, sweet Rādhikā! Ah, beloved of the Lord of my life! Alas, where is the enchantress of the flute player, the moon-faced queen of my life? Alas, where is *rasa* personified, the beauty of Vṛndāvana?' Is this not wonderful?

TEXT 8

हे राधाप्रिय राधिकादयित हे गोविन्द गोपीपते
हे वृन्दावनसुन्दरो रमण हे हा प्राणनाथः कुतः ।
इत्थं प्रेमसुधारसं सुमधुरं पित्वा प्रमत्तं जगद्
गौडे गौरसुधाकरे समुदिते किं किं विचित्रं न हि ॥ ८ ॥

he rādhā-priya rādhikā-dayita he govinda gopīpate
he vṛndāvana-sundaro ramaṇa he hā prāṇa-nāthaḥ kutaḥ |
itthaṁ prema-sudhā-rasaṁ su-madhuraṁ pitvā pramattaṁ jagad
gauḍe gaura-sudhākare samudite kiṁ kiṁ vicitraṁ na hi || 8 ||

Word-For-Word Meanings

he rādhā-priya – O beloved of Rādhā; *rādhikā-dayita* – O lover of Rādhikā; *he govinda* – O Govinda; *gopīpate* – O Lord of the *gopīs*; *he* – O; *vṛndāvana-sundaraḥ* – the beauty of Vṛndāvana; *ramaṇa* – O charming One; *he* – O; *hā* – alas; *prāṇa-nāthaḥ* – the Lord of my life; *kutaḥ* – where; *ittham* – thus; *prema-sudhā-rasam* – the nectarean *rasa* of love of God; *su-madhuram* – very sweet; *pitvā* – having drunk; *pramattam* – intoxicated; *jagat* – the world; *gauḍe* – in Gauḍadeśa; *gaura-sudhākare* – moon-like Gaurāṅga; *samudite* – having appeared; *kiṁ kim* – what; *vicitram* – wonderful; *na* – not; *hi* – indeed.

Translation

As the moon-like Lord Gaurāṅga appeared in Gauḍadeśa, having drunk the very sweet nectarean *rasa* of love of God, the whole world is intoxicated and is repeatedly murmuring thus: 'O beloved of Rādhā! O lover of Rādhikā! O Govinda! O Lord of the *gopīs*! O charming One! Alas, where is the beauty of Vṛndāvana? Alas, where is the Lord of my life?' Is this not wonderful?

TEXT 9

यैरेतत्पठितं सुनिर्मलधिया चैतन्यचित्राष्टकं
श्रुत्वा वा मनसा गृणन्ति विवशा गायन्ति येऽहर्निशम् ।
सर्वे पापसुदुष्कृतिं च विनशन्मज्जन्ति प्रेमाम्बुधा-
वन्ते तस्य पदारविन्दयुगले तिष्ठन्ति मा संशयः ॥ ९ ॥

yair etat paṭhitaṁ su-nirmala-dhiyā caitanya-citrāṣṭakaṁ
śrutvā vā manasā gṛṇanti vivaśā gāyanti ye 'har-niśam |
sarve pāpa-suduṣkṛtiṁ ca vinaśan majjanti premāmbudhāv
ante tasya padāravinda-yugale tiṣṭhanti mā saṁśayaḥ || 9 ||

Word-For-Word Meanings

yaiḥ – by whom; *etat* – this; *paṭhitam* – is read; *su-nirmala-dhiyā* – with a very pure mind; *caitanya-citrāṣṭakam* – eight verses glorifying Lord Caitanya; *śrutvā* – having heard; *vā* – or; *manasā* – with the heart; *gṛṇanti* – accept; *vivaśāḥ* – helpless; *gāyanti* – sing; *ye* – those who; *ahar-niśam* – day and night; *sarve* – all; *pāpa-suduṣkṛtim* – offenses and sins; *ca* – and; *vinaśat* – being destroyed; *majjanti* – become immersed; *premāmbudhau* – in the ocean of love of God;

ante – finally; *tasya* – His; *padāravinda-yugale* – at the lotus feet; *tiṣṭhanti* – remain; *mā* – not; *saṁśayaḥ* – doubt.

Translation

Those who read this *Caitanya-citrāṣṭakam* with a very pure mind, and those helpless souls who having heard it, accept it within the heart and sing it day and night, will all become immersed in the ocean of love of God, while their offenses and sins are gradually destroyed, and finally they remain at the lotus feet of Lord Caitanya. There is no doubt about this.

iti śrīmat-prabodhānanda-sarasvatī-viracitaṁ śrī-caitanya-citrāṣṭakaṁ sampūrṇam ||

Thus ends the *Śrī Caitanya-citrāṣṭakam* composed by Śrīla Prabodhānanda Sarasvatī.

Śrī-Nityānandāṣṭakam

TEXT 1

शरच्चन्द्रभ्रान्तिस्फुरदमलकान्तिं गजगतिं
हरिप्रेमोन्मत्तं धृतपरमसत्त्वं स्मितमुखम् ।
समाघूर्णन्नेत्रं करकलितवेत्रं कलिभिदं
भजे नित्यानन्दं भजनतरुकन्दं निरवधि ॥ १ ॥

śarac-candra-bhrānti-sphurad-amala-kāntiṁ gaja-gatiṁ
hari-premonmattaṁ dhṛta-parama-sattvaṁ smita-mukham |
samāghūrṇan-netraṁ kara-kalita-vetraṁ kali-bhidaṁ
bhaje nityānandaṁ bhajana-taru-kandaṁ niravadhi || 1 ||

Word-for-word Meanings

śarac-candra – the autumn moon; *bhrānti* – bewilderment; *sphurat* – shining; *amala* – spotless; *kāntim* – beauty; *gaja-gatim* – elephant gait; *hari* – for Lord Hari; *prema* – of love; *unmattam* – intoxicated; *dhṛta-parama-sattvam* – holding the supreme truth; *smita-mukham* – smiling face; *samāghūrṇan-netram* – rolling eyes; *kara-kalita-vetram* – carrying a stick in His hands; *kali-bhidam* – breaking Kali; *bhaje* – I worship; *nityānandam* – Lord Nityānanda; *bhajana-taru-kandam* – the root of the tree of devotional service; *niravadhi* – always.

Translation

His shining spotless beauty bewilders the autumn moon. With a smiling face and rolling eyes, intoxicated with love for Lord Hari, He walks like an elephant. He holds the supreme truth and carries a stick that breaks the effects of Kali-yuga. I always worship Lord Nityānanda, the root of the tree of devotional service.

TEXT 2

रसानामासारं स्वजनगणसर्वस्वमतुलं
तदीयैकप्राणप्रतिमवसुधाजाह्नविपतिम् ।
सदा प्रेमोन्मादं परमविदितं मन्दमनसां
भजे नित्यानन्दं भजनतरुकन्दं निरवधि ॥ २ ॥

rasānām āsāraṁ sva-jana-gaṇa-sarvasvam atulaṁ
tadīyaika-prāṇa-pratima-vasudhā-jāhnavi-patim |
sadā premonmādaṁ param aviditaṁ manda-manasāṁ
bhaje nityānandaṁ bhajana-taru-kandaṁ niravadhi || 2 ||

Word-for-word Meanings

rasānām – of *rasas*; *āsāram* – a shower; *sva-jana-gaṇa-sarvasvam* – the all in all for His devotees; *atulam* – incomparable; *tadīyaika-prāṇa-pratima* – like their very life; *vasudhā-jāhnavi-patim* – the husband of Vasudhā and Jāhnavī; *sadā* – always; *premonmādam* – mad with love; *param* – but; *aviditam* – unknown; *manda-manasām* – to those whose minds are dull; *bhaje* – I worship; *nityānandam* – Lord Nityānanda; *bhajana-taru- kandam* – the root of the tree of devotional service; *niravadhi* – always.

Translation

He is the husband of Vasudhā and Jāhnavī, and their life and soul. Always mad with love for God, He is incomparable and a shower of transcendental *rasas.* He is the all in all for His devotees but is unknown to the fools. I always worship Lord Nityānanda, the root of the tree of devotional service.

TEXT 3

शचीसूनुप्रेष्ठं निखिलजगदिष्टं सुखमयं
कलौ मज्जज्जीवोद्धरणकरणोद्दामकरुणम् ।
हरेराख्यानाद्वा भवजलधिगर्वोन्नतिहरं
भजे नित्यानन्दं भजनतरुकन्दं निरवधि ॥ ३ ॥

śacī-sūnu-preṣṭhaṁ nikhila-jagad-iṣṭaṁ sukha-mayaṁ
kalau majjaj-jīvoddharaṇa-karaṇoddāma-karuṇam |
harer ākhyānād vā bhava-jaladhi-garvonnati-haraṁ
bhaje nityānandaṁ bhajana-taru-kandaṁ niravadhi || 3 ||

Word-for-word Meanings

śacī-sūnu-preṣṭham – the dearest of the son of Śacī; *nikhila-jagad-iṣṭam* – worshipped by the whole universe; *sukha-mayam* – bliss personified; *kalau* – in Kali-yuga; *majjaj-jīvoddharaṇa* – for saving the drowning souls; *karaṇoddāma-karuṇam* – whose unlimited mercy is the cause; *hareḥ* – of Lord Hari; *ākhyānāt* – by preaching; *vā* – and; *bhava-jaladhi-garvonnati-haram* – removing the rising pride of the ocean of material existence; *bhaje* – I worship; *nityānandam* – Lord Nityānanda; *bhajana-taru-kandam* – the root of the tree of devotional service; *niravadhi* – always.

Translation

He is worshipped by the whole universe and is the dearest associate of the son of mother Śacī. He is bliss personified and His unlimited mercy is the cause of salvation for the souls drowning in the ocean of Kali. By preaching the glories of Lord Hari, He removes the rising pride of the ocean of material existence. I always worship Lord Nityānanda, the root of the tree of devotional service.

TEXT 4

अये भ्रातर्नृणां कलिकलुषिणां किं नु भविता
तथा प्रायश्चित्तं रचय यदनायासत इमे।
व्रजन्ति त्वामित्थं सह भगवता मन्त्रयति यो
भजे नित्यानन्दं भजनतरुकन्दं निरवधि ॥ ४ ॥

aye bhrātar nṛṇāṁ kali-kaluṣiṇāṁ kiṁ nu bhavitā
tathā prāyaścittaṁ racaya yad anāyāsata ime |
vrajanti tvām itthaṁ saha bhagavatā mantrayati yo
bhaje nityānandaṁ bhajana-taru-kandaṁ niravadhi || 4 ||

Word-for-word Meanings

aye bhrātaḥ – O brother; *nṛṇām* – to the people; *kali-kaluṣiṇām* – contaminated by Kali; *kiṁ nu* – what; *bhavitā* – will happen; *tathā* – such; *prāyaścittam* – atonement; *racaya* – arrange; *yat* – so that; *anāyāsataḥ* – easily; *ime* – these; *vrajanti* – go; *tvām* – to You; *ittham* – thus; *saha* – with; *bhagavatā* – the Supreme Lord (Caitanya); *mantrayati* – speaks; *yaḥ* – Who; *bhaje* – I worship; *nityānandam* – Lord

Nityānanda; *bhajana-taru-kandam* – the root of the tree of devotional service; *niravadhi* – always.

Translation

"O brother, what will happen to these people contaminated by the Age of Kali? Please arrange a process of atonement so that they may easily go to You." I always worship Lord Nityānanda, the root of the tree of devotional service, Who speaks to Lord Caitanya in this way.

TEXT 5

यथेष्टं रे भ्रातः कुरु हरिहरिध्वानमनिशं
ततो वः संसाराम्बुधितरणदायो मयि लगेत् ।
इदं बाहुस्फोटैरटति विरटन् यः प्रतिगृहं
भजे नित्यानन्दं भजनतरुकन्दं निरवधि ॥ ५ ॥

yatheṣṭaṁ re bhrātaḥ kuru hari-hari-dhvānam aniśaṁ
tato vaḥ saṁsārāmbudhi-taraṇa-dāyo mayi laget |
idaṁ bāhu-sphoṭair aṭati viraṭan yaḥ pratigṛhaṁ
bhaje nityānandaṁ bhajana-taru-kandaṁ niravadhi || 5 ||

Word-for-word Meanings

yatheṣṭam – according to His own will; *re bhrātaḥ* – O brother; *kuru* – do; *hari-hari-dhvānam* – the sound "Hari, Hari;" *aniśam* – incessantly; *tataḥ* – therefore; *vaḥ* – your; *saṁsārāmbudhi-taraṇa-dāyaḥ* – a charity in the form of crossing the ocean of birth and death; *mayi* – to Me; *laget* – bestow; *idam* – this; *bāhu-sphoṭaiḥ* – with raised arms; *aṭati* – roams; *viraṭan* – shouting; *yaḥ* – Who; *pratigṛham* –

at every house; *bhaje* – I worship; *nityānandam* – Lord Nityānanda; *bhajana-taru-kandam* – the root of the tree of devotional service; *niravadhi* – always.

Translation

According to His own will, He went from house to house shouting with raised arms, "O brother, incessantly chant 'Hari, Hari' and in this way you will cross the ocean of birth and death. Please give me such a charity." I always worship Lord Nityānanda, the root of the tree of devotional service.

TEXT 6

नटन्तं गायन्तं हरिमनुवदन्तं पथि पथि
व्रजन्तं पश्यन्तं स्वमपि सुदुरन्तं जनगणम् ।
प्रकुर्वन्तं सन्तं करुणसुदृगन्तं प्रवलनाद्
भजे नित्यानन्दं भजनतरुकन्दं निरवधि ॥ ६ ॥

naṭantaṁ gāyantaṁ harim anuvadantaṁ pathi pathi
vrajantaṁ paśyantaṁ svam api sudurantaṁ jana-gaṇam |
prakurvantaṁ santaṁ karuṇa-sudṛg-antaṁ pravalanād
bhaje nityānandaṁ bhajana-taru-kandaṁ niravadhi || 6 ||

Word-for-word Meanings

naṭantam – dancing; *gāyantam* – singing; *harim* – Lord Hari; *anuvadantam* – repeatedly saying; *pathi pathi* – in every road; *vrajantam* – moving along; *paśyantam* – looking; *svam* – Himself; *api* – and; *sudur-antam* – endless; *jana-gaṇam* – group of people; *prakurvantam* – doing;

santam – saintly; *karuṇa-sudṛg-antam* – the corner of His beautiful eyes, which are full of compassion; *pravalanāt* – by turning around; *bhaje* – I worship; *nityānandam* – Lord Nityānanda; *bhajana-taru-kandam* – the root of the tree of devotional service; *niravadhi* – always.

Translation

Repeatedly saying "Hari, Hari," He was dancing and chanting along every road. He would see endless saintly persons approaching Him, and by turning around He would cast His compassionate side-glances upon them from the corner of His beautiful eyes. I always worship Lord Nityānanda, the root of the tree of devotional service.

TEXT 7

बलात्संसाराम्भोनिधिहरणकुम्भोद्भवमहो
सतां श्रेयःसिन्धून्नतिकुमुदबन्धुं समुदितम् ।
खलश्रेणीस्फूर्जत्तिमिरहरसूर्यप्रभमहं
भजे नित्यानन्दं भजनतरुकन्दं निरवधि ॥ ७ ॥

balāt saṁsārāmbhonidhi-haraṇa-kumbhodbhavam aho
satāṁ śreyaḥ-sindhūnnati-kumuda-bandhuṁ samuditam |
khala-śreṇī-sphūrjat-timira-hara-sūrya-prabham ahaṁ
bhaje nityānandaṁ bhajana-taru-kandaṁ niravadhi || 7 ||

Word-for-word Meanings

balāt – forcibly; *saṁsārāmbhonidhi-haraṇa* – annihilating the ocean of material existence; *kumbhodbhavam* – like Agastya Muni; *aho* – oh; *satām* – of saintly persons;

śreyaḥ-sindhūnnati – increasing the ocean of happiness; *kumuda-bandhum* – the moon; *samuditam* – risen; *khala-śreṇī* – groups of rogues; *sphūrjat-timira-hara* – removing the expanding darkness; *sūrya-prabham* – radiance of the sun; *aham* – I; *bhaje* – I worship; *nityānandam* – Lord Nityānanda; *bhajana-taru-kandam* – the root of the tree of devotional service; *niravadhi* – always.

Translation

Like Agastya Muni, He forcibly annihilates the ocean of material existence.[1] He is like a risen moon increasing the ocean of happiness for the saintly persons. He is similar to the radiance of the sun dissipating darkness-like rogues. I always worship Lord Nityānanda, the root of the tree of devotional service.

TEXT 8

सुबिभ्राणं भ्रातुः करसरसिजं कोमलतरं
मिथो वक्त्रालोकोच्चलितपरमानन्दहृदयम् ।
भ्रमन्तं माधुर्यैरहह मदयन्तं पुरजनान्
भजे नित्यानन्दं भजनतरुकन्दं निरवधि ॥ ८ ॥

subibhrāṇaṁ bhrātuḥ kara-sarasijaṁ komalataraṁ
mitho vaktrālokoccalita-paramānanda-hṛdayam |

1. The *Mahābhārata* (Vana-parva, chapters 100-104) narrates how Agastya Muni, who was born from a pitcher (*kumbhodbhava*), swallowed the ocean. Here the author glorifies Lord Nityānanda by comparing Him with Agastya Muni, for He is able to make the whole ocean of miseries dry.

bhramantaṁ mādhuryair ahaha madayantaṁ pura-janān
bhaje nityānandaṁ bhajana-taru-kandaṁ niravadhi || 8 ||

Word-for-word Meanings

subibhrāṇam – holding; *bhrātuḥ* – of His brother (Nimāi); *kara- sarasijam* – lotus hand; *komalataram* – very soft; *mithaḥ* – at each other; *vaktrāloka* – by glancing at the face; *uccalita-paramānanda-hṛdayam* – Whose heart is full of increasing transcendental bliss; *bhramantam* – roaming about; *mādhuryaiḥ* – with sweetness; *ahaha* – oh; *madayantam* – delighting; *pura-janān* – the residents of the towns; *bhaje* – I worship; *nityānandam* – Lord Nityānanda; *bhajana-taru-kandam* – the root of the tree of devotional service; *niravadhi* – always.

Translation

Oh! Holding the very soft lotus hand of His brother Nimāi, His heart full of increasing transcendental bliss by glancing at each other's face, He roams about delighting the people with His sweetness. I always worship Lord Nityānanda, the root of the tree of devotional service.

TEXT 9

सुखानामाधानं रसिकवरसद्वैष्णवधनं
रसागारं सारं पतिततितारं स्मरणतः ।
परं नित्यानन्दाष्टकमिदमपूर्वं पठति यस्
तदंघ्रिद्वन्द्वाब्जं स्फुरतु नितरां तस्य हृदये ॥ ९ ॥

sukhānām ādhānaṁ rasika-vara-sad-vaiṣṇava-dhanaṁ
rasāgāraṁ sāraṁ patita-tati-tāraṁ smaraṇataḥ |

paraṁ nityānandāṣṭakam idam apūrvaṁ paṭhati yas
tad-aṅghri-dvandvābjaṁ sphuratu nitarāṁ tasya hṛdaye || 9 ||

Word-for-word Meanings

sukhānām – of all happiness; *ādhānam* – reservoir; *rasika-vara-sad-vaiṣṇava-dhanam* – the treasure of saintly Vaiṣṇavas and best of *rasikas*; *rasāgāram* – the repository of *rasa*; *sāram* – the essence; *patita-tati- tāram* – the saviour of multitudes of fallen souls; *smaraṇataḥ* – by remembering; *param* – transcendental; *nityānandāṣṭakam* – eight verses in praise of Lord Nityānanda; *idam* – this; *apūrvam* – unprecedented; *paṭhati* – reads; *yaḥ* – one who; *tad-aṅghri-dvandvābjam* – His lotus feet; *sphuratu* – may become manifest; *nitarām* – always; *tasya* – his; *hṛdaye* – in the heart.

Translation

May Lord Nityānanda's lotus feet become always manifest in the heart of one who reads this transcendental and unprecedented *Nityānandāṣṭakam,* which is the reservoir of all happiness, the treasure of saintly Vaiṣṇavas and best of *rasikas,* the repository of *rasa,* and the essence. Multitudes of fallen souls can be saved by simply remembering it.

iti śrī-prabodhānanda-sarasvatī-viracitaṁ śrī-nityānandāṣṭakaṁ samāptam ||

Thus ends the *Śrī Nityānandāṣṭakam* composed by Śrīla Prabodhānanda Sarasvatī.

Viveka-śatakam

A Hundred Verses of Wisdom

TEXT 1

देहः प्राप्तो विरसजरसं क्षीणमायुर्ममाभूत्
स्वल्पा शक्तिर्विषमविषयग्राहिणी येन्द्रियाणाम् ।
दूरे वृन्दावनतटभुवः खेदभेदप्रदायाः
किं कुर्वेऽहं व्रजकुलशिरोरत्नयत्नं न वेद्मि ॥ १ ॥

dehaḥ prāpto virasa-jarasaṁ kṣīṇam āyur mamābhūt
svalpā śaktir viṣama-viṣaya-grāhiṇī yendriyāṇām |
dūre vṛndāvana-taṭa-bhuvaḥ kheda-bheda-pradāyāḥ
kiṁ kurve 'haṁ vraja-kula-śiro-ratna-yatnaṁ na vedmi || 1 ||

Word-For-Word Meanings

dehaḥ – the body; *prāptaḥ* – attained; *virasa-jarasam* – the unpleasant state of old age; *kṣīṇam* – reduced; *āyuḥ* – life span; *mama* – my; *abhūt* – has become; *su-alpā* – very little; *śaktiḥ* – strength; *viṣama-viṣaya- grāhiṇī* – grasping strong sense objects; *yā* – which; *indriyāṇām* – of the senses; *dūre* – far away; *vṛndāvana-taṭa-bhuvaḥ* – the lands of Vṛndāvana; *kheda-bheda-pradāyāḥ* – which remove distress; *kim* – what; *kurve* – I do; *aham* – I; *vraja-kula-śiro-ratna-yatnam* – endeavour for the crest jewel of the residents of Vraja; *na* – not; *vedmi* – know.

Translation

My body has attained the unpleasant state of old age, my life span is reduced, and my senses have little strength to grasp strong sense objects. What shall I do? The lands of Vṛndāvana, which remove all distress, are situated far away, and I do not know how to endeavour for the crest jewel of the residents of Vraja.

TEXT 2

अहं सागो मागास्त्वमपि भगवन्मन्तुगणनां
यतो भृत्यः कृत्यं तव किमपि जाने न सपदि ।
सुहृत्ता हृत्तापं हरति भवतः सर्वविदितं
जनो मूढोऽगूढां तदपि सखितां ते न मनुते ॥ २ ॥

ahaṁ sāgo māgās tvam api bhagavan mantu-gaṇanāṁ
yato bhṛtyaḥ kṛtyaṁ tava kim api jāne na sapadi |
suhṛttā hṛt-tāpaṁ harati bhavataḥ sarva-viditaṁ
jano mūḍho 'gūḍhāṁ tad api sakhitāṁ te na manute || 2 ||

Word-For-Word Meanings

aham – I; *sa-āgaḥ* – guilty; *mā* – do not; *agāḥ* – go; *tvam* – You; *api* – also; *bhagavan* – O Lord; *mantu-gaṇanām* – counting the faults; *yataḥ* – because; *bhṛtyaḥ* – servant; *kṛtyam* – what should be done; *tava* – Your; *kim api* – anything; *jāne* – know; *na* – not; *sapadi* – quickly; *suhṛttā* – friendship; *hṛt-tāpam* – the pain in the heart; *harati* – removes; *bhavataḥ* – to You; *sarva-viditam* – all known; *janaḥ* – a person; *mūḍhaḥ* – foolish; *agūḍhām* – unreserved;

tat api – yet; *sakhitām* – friendship; *te* – Your; *na* – not; *manute* – regard;

Translation

O my dear Lord, although I am guilty, please do not take my faults into consideration, for I am Your servant and have no idea about what should be done. Friendship with You quickly removes the pain in one's heart, which is all known to You. Yet a foolish person does not regard Your unreserved friendship.

TEXT 3

शरीरं ते दत्तं निजभजनहेतोरविकलं
कृतावृत्तिः पूर्णा त्रिजगति सतो मातुरुदरे ।
मया सर्वं नाथ त्वदुपकरणं विस्मृतमभून्
ममैतद्यद् दुःखं तदतिलघु नागोऽनुसरति ॥ ३ ॥

śarīraṁ te dattaṁ nija-bhajana-hetor avikalaṁ
kṛtāvṛttiḥ pūrṇā tri-jagati sato mātur udare |
mayā sarvaṁ nātha tvad-upakaraṇaṁ vismṛtam abhūn
mamaitad yad duḥkhaṁ tad ati-laghu nāgo 'nusarati || 3 ||

Word-For-Word Meanings

śarīram – body; *te* – by You; *dattam* – given; *nija-bhajana-hetoḥ* – for the purpose of worshipping You; *avikalam* – perfect; *kṛtā* - done; *āvṛttiḥ* – cycle of birth and death; *pūrṇā* – complete; *tri-jagati* – in the three worlds; *sataḥ* – for anyone existing; *mātuḥ* – of the mother; *udare* – in the womb; *mayā* – by me; *sarvam* – everything; *nātha* – O Lord;

tvad-upakaraṇam – Your help; *vismṛtam* – forgotten; *abhūt* – was; *mama* – my; e*tat* – this; *yat* – which; *duḥkham* – suffering; *tat* – that; *ati-laghu* – very small; *na* – not; *āgaḥ* – sin; *anusarati* – befits.

Translation

After a living entity has gone through a complete cycle of birth and death in the three worlds, this perfect human body is given by You within the womb of a mother for the purpose of worshipping You. O Lord, I have completely forgotten all the help I received from You. My suffering is actually very small compared to what befits my offenses.

TEXT 4

अत्यल्पोदरपूरणाय कुधिया विक्रीतमायुर्मया
श्रीकृष्णं जगदेकपालनपरं त्यक्त्वा नृपाणां करे ।
द्वारि द्वारि पराभवानुभवतो दुःखं समासादितं
येनादायि तनुर्नरस्य भगवान् देवः स मे विस्मृतः ॥ ४ ॥

aty-alpodara-pūraṇāya kudhiyā vikrītam āyur mayā
śrī-kṛṣṇaṁ jagad-eka-pālana-paraṁ tyaktvā nṛpāṇāṁ kare |
dvāri dvāri parābhavānubhavato duḥkhaṁ samāsāditaṁ
yenādāyi tanur narasya bhagavān devaḥ sa me vismṛtaḥ || 4 ||

Word-For-Word Meanings

aty-alpodara-pūraṇāya – for filling a tiny belly; *ku-dhiyā* – by this fool; *vikrītam* – sold out; *āyuḥ* – life span; *mayā* – by me; *śrī-kṛṣṇam* – to Lord Kṛṣṇa; *jagad-eka-pālana-param* – the sole protector of the universe; *tyaktvā* – having given up; *nṛpāṇām* – of kings; *kare* – in the hand; *dvāri dvāri* – at every door; *parābhavānubhavataḥ* – by experiencing humiliation; *duḥkham* – suffering; *samāsāditam* – overtaken; *yena* – by which; *adāyi* – given; *tanuḥ* – body; *narasya* – of man; *bhagavān* – the Supreme Lord; *devaḥ* – God; *saḥ* – He; *me* – by me; *vismṛtaḥ* – forgotten.

Translation

I am such a fool that I sold out my life just to fill my tiny belly. Giving up Lord Kṛṣṇa, the sole protector of the whole universe, I fell into the hands of kings. Experiencing humiliation from door to door, suffering overtook me. The Supreme Lord, Who gave me this human body, was forgotten by me.

TEXT 5

मग्नाः सम्प्रति बन्धुकृत्यजलधौ किं कुर्महे दुर्धियो
नौरस्माभिरनाश्रिता मधुपुरी यत्कर्णधारो हरिः ।
लोभग्राहमुखान्तरालपतितानस्मान् विना केशवं
रक्षेद्यः सकृपः स एव भगवान् भक्तेष्वभक्तेष्वपि ॥ ५ ॥

magnāḥ samprati bandhu-kṛtya-jaladhau kiṁ kurmahe durdhiyo
naur asmābhir anāśritā madhupurī yat-karṇa-dhāro hariḥ |
lobha-grāha-mukhāntarāla-patitān asmān vinā keśavaṁ
rakṣed yaḥ sa-kṛpaḥ sa eva bhagavān bhakteṣv abhakteṣv api || 5 ||

Word-For-Word Meanings

magnāḥ – immersed; *samprati* – now; *bandhu-kṛtya-jaladhau* – in the ocean of service to relatives; *kim* – what;

kurmahe – we do; *dur-dhiyaḥ* – fools; *nauḥ* – boat; *asmābhiḥ* – by us; *anāśritā* – not having taken shelter; *madhupurī* – Mathurā; *yat-karṇa-dhāraḥ* – whose boatman; *hariḥ* – Lord Hari; *lobha-grāha-mukhāntarāla-patitān* – fallen into the mouth of an alligator whose form is greed; *asmān* – to us; *vinā* – without; *keśavam* – Lord Keśava; *rakṣet* – can protect; *yaḥ* – He Who; *sa-kṛpaḥ* – merciful; *saḥ* – He; *eva* – only; *bhagavān* – the Supreme Lord; *bhakteṣu* – towards devotees; *abhakteṣu* – towards non-devotees; *api* – as well.

Translation

Being now immersed in the ocean of service to relatives, we fools have not taken shelter in Mathurā, which is like a boat whose boatman is Lord Hari. Without Lord Keśava, we have fallen into the mouth of an alligator whose form is greed. Only that Supreme Lord, Who is merciful both to devotees as well as to non-devotees, can protect us.

TEXT 6

बाल्ये दुर्मतिरेव मे समभवत् को वेद तीर्थाटनं
तारुण्ये विषयेच्छुना क्षितिभुजां द्वारि स्थितं नीचवत् ।
ग्रस्तेयं जरसैव सम्प्रति तनुर्ध्वस्तेन्द्रियाणां क्रिया-
पाशः स्नेहमयो गले निपतितः क्वाहं क्व वृन्दावनम् ॥ ६ ॥

bālye durmatir eva me samabhavat ko veda tīrthāṭanaṁ
tāruṇye viṣayecchunā kṣiti-bhujāṁ dvāri sthitaṁ nīcavat |
grasteyaṁ jarasaiva samprati tanur dhvastendriyāṇāṁ kriyā-
pāśaḥ sneha-mayo gale nipatitaḥ kvāhaṁ kva vṛndāvanam || 6 ||

Word-For-Word Meanings

bālye – in childhood; *dur-matiḥ* – bad intelligence; *eva* – indeed; *me* – my; *samabhavat* – became; *kaḥ* – who; *veda* – knows; *tīrthāṭanam* – pilgrimage in holy places; *tāruṇye* – in youth; *viṣayecchunā* – with desire for sense gratification; *kṣiti-bhujām* – of kings; *dvāri* – at the door; *sthitam* – standing; *nīcavat* – like an inferior; *grastā* – taken over; *iyam* – this; *jarasā* – by decrepitude; *eva* – indeed; *samprati* – now; *tanuḥ* – body; *dhvastendriyāṇām* – of the destroyed sense organs; *kriyā-pāśaḥ* – the noose of activities; *sneha-mayaḥ* – in the form of affection; *gale* – on the neck; *nipatitaḥ* – placed; *kva* – where; *aham* – I; *kva* – where; *vṛndāvanam* – Vṛndāvana.

Translation

In childhood I was already a fool; after all, at that age who knows what pilgrimage to a holy place is? In my youth, filled with desire for sense gratification, I was standing at the doors of kings like an inferior. Now this body is already taken over by decrepitude, but although my sense organs are destroyed, the noose of their activities remains tight around my neck in the form of affection. Alas, how far I am from Vṛndāvana!

TEXT 7

मद्धस्तार्पितराजहस्तजनितो गर्वो ग्रसन्मे मतिं
तस्याग्रासनसंस्थितिर्नयनयोश्चक्रे दृढामावृतिम् ।
तद्दत्तेन धनेन साधु शिरसि न्यस्तं पदं तन्मया
नागः किं किमकारि नाथ भवते यद्रोचते तत् कुरु ॥ ७ ॥

mad-dhastārpita-rāja-hasta-janito garvo grasan me matiṁ
tasyāgrāsana-saṁsthitir nayanayoś cakre dṛḍhām āvṛtim |
tad-dattena dhanena sādhu śirasi nyastaṁ padaṁ tan mayā
nāgaḥ kiṁ kim akāri nātha bhavate yad rocate tat kuru || 7 ||

Word-For-Word Meanings

mad-dhastārpita-rāja-hasta-janitaḥ – produced by having the hands of kings placed on my hands; *garvaḥ* – pride; *grasan* – devouring; *me* – my; *matim* – heart; *tasya* – its; *agrāsana-saṁsthitiḥ* – resting on a distinct seat; *nayanayoḥ* – for the eyes; *cakre* – created; *dṛḍhām* – strong; *āvṛtim* – cover; *tad-dattena* – given by them; *dhanena* – by the wealth; *sādhu* – well; *śirasi* – on the head; *nyastam* – placed; *padam* – a foot; *tat* – that; *mayā* – by me; *na* – not; *āgaḥ* – sin; *kiṁ kim* – what; *akāri* – done; *nātha* – O Lord; *bhavato* – to You; *yat* – whatever; *rocate* – pleases; *tat* – that; *kuru* – do.

Translation

The pride of having the hands of kings placed on my hands has created a strong covering over my eyes, is devouring my heart and occupies a distinct place in it. The wealth given by them is like a foot well placed on my head. What sin have I not committed? My Lord, now do as You please.

TEXT 8

यतः प्रभृति नाथ ते चरणपङ्कजं त्यक्तवान्
अनन्त तव मायया गहनगर्वकूपेऽपतम् ।

ततः कृतमनेकधा दुरितमीश नान्यत् कृतं
यथारुचि कुरु क्षमे पुनरनुग्रहं निग्रहम् ॥ ८ ॥

yataḥ prabhṛti nātha te caraṇa-paṅkajaṁ tyaktavān
ananta tava māyayā gahana-garva-kūpe 'patam |
tataḥ kṛtam anekadhā duritam īśa nānyat kṛtaṁ
yathā-ruci kuru kṣame punar anugrahaṁ nigraham || 8 ||

Word-For-Word Meanings

yataḥ prabhṛti – since when; *nātha* – O Lord; *te* – Your; *caraṇa-paṅkajam* – lotus feet; *tyaktavān* – gave up; *ananta* – O unlimited One; *tava* – Your; *māyayā* – by *māyā*; *gahana-garva-kūpe* – into the deep well of pride; *apatam* – I fell down; *tataḥ* – since then; *kṛtam* – done; *anekadhā* – many kinds; *duritam* – sin; *īśa* – O Lord; *na* – not; *anyat* – something else; *kṛtam* – done; *yathā-ruci* – as You wish; *kuru* – do; *kṣame* – in a befitting manner; *punaḥ* – again; *anugraham* – favour; *nigraham* – punishment.

Translation

My Lord, since I gave up Your lotus feet, I fell down into the deep well of pride by the influence of Your illusory energy, O Ananta, and have committed many kinds of sinful deeds and nothing else. O Lord, punish me in a befitting manner as You wish, but then again show me Your favour.

TEXT 9

नश्यत्युत्कटसंसृतिर्न सदने सक्तस्य पुंसोऽशुभा
सत्सङ्गेन विनापि नाकिनमपि ग्रासीकरोत्येव सा ।

तस्माद्गन्तुमितः कलिन्दतनयातीरस्थवृन्दावनं
हस्तं नाथ गृहाण मे करुणया दीनस्य दैन्यं हर ॥ ९ ॥

naśyaty utkaṭa-saṁsṛtir na sadane saktasya puṁso 'śubhā
sat-saṅgena vināpi nākinam api grāsī-karoty eva sā |
tasmād gantum itaḥ kalinda-tanayā-tīra-stha-vṛndāvanaṁ
hastaṁ nātha gṛhāṇa me karuṇayā dīnasya dainyaṁ hara || 9 ||

Word-For-Word Meanings

naśyati – disappears; *utkaṭa-saṁsṛtiḥ* – formidable wordly life; *na* – not; *sadane* – in the house; *saktasya* – attached; *puṁsaḥ – of a man; aśubhā* – inauspicious; *sat-saṅgena* – association of saintly persons; *vinā* – without; *api* – also; *nākinam* – a denizen of heaven; *api* – even; *grāsī-karoti* – swallows; *eva* – certainly; *sā* – that; *tasmāt* – therefore; *gantum* – to go; *itaḥ* – from here; *kalinda-tanayā-tīra-stha-vṛndāvanam* – to Vṛndāvana, which is situated on the banks of the Yamunā; *hastam* – hand; *nātha* – O Lord; *gṛhāṇa* – catch; *me* – my; *karuṇayā* – mercifully; *dīnasya* – of this wretch; *dainyam* – dejection; *hara* – remove.

Translation

The formidable inauspicious worldly life swallows even the denizens of heaven, and it certainly never disappears from the house of an attached man without the association of saintly persons. Therefore, O Lord, please remove my dejection and mercifully catch the hand of this wretch so that I may leave this place and go to Vṛndāvana, situated on the banks of the Yamunā.

TEXT 10

दग्धोऽहं विषयाग्निना निपतितः संसारगर्तेऽधुना
दष्टः क्रोधमहाहिना गतमतिर्निर्गन्तुमिच्छन्नितः।
पश्याम्यत्र विना न गोकुलपते त्वां हस्तसङ्ग्राहकं
दीनाः के विधिशक्रशर्वदिनकृन्मुख्याश्च यानर्थये ॥ १०॥

dagdho 'haṁ viṣayāgninā nipatitaḥ saṁsāra-garte 'dhunā
daṣṭaḥ krodha-mahāhinā gata-matir nirgantum icchann itaḥ |
paśyāmy atra vinā na gokula-pate tvāṁ hasta-saṅgrāhakaṁ
dīnāḥ ke vidhi-śakra-śarva-dinakṛn-mukhyāś ca yān arthaye ||10||

Word-For-Word Meanings

dagdhaḥ – burnt; *aham* – I; *viṣayāgninā* – by the fire of sense objects; *nipatitaḥ* – fallen; *saṁsāra-garte* – into the pit of material existence; *adhunā* – now; *daṣṭaḥ* – bitten; *krodha-mahāhinā* – by the snake of anger; *gata-matiḥ* – devoid of intelligence; *nirgantum* – to get out; *icchan* – desiring; *itaḥ* – from here; *paśyāmi* – I see; *atra* – here; *vinā* – except; *na* – not; *gokula-pate* – O Lord of Gokula; *tvām* – You; *hasta-saṅgrāhakam* – catching my hand; *dīnāḥ* – poor; *ke* – who; *vidhi-śakra-śarva-dinakṛn-mukhyāḥ* – demigods headed by Brahmā, Indra, Śiva, Sūrya, etc.; *ca* – and; *yān* – to whom; *arthaye* – I pray.

Translation

Being devoid of intelligence, I have fallen into the pit of material existence and now I am burnt by the fire of sense objects and bitten by the great snake of anger. O Lord of Gokula, desiring to get out of here, I do not see anyone who could catch my hand except You. Who are these poor Brahmā, Indra, Śiva, Sūrya, and others to whom I pray?

TEXT 11

क्वेदं कलेवरमनेकरुजां निदानम्
अन्तेऽपि यस्य कृमिभस्मपुरीषसंज्ञाः ।
तस्मिन् विधाय कुधियो ममतामहन्तां
त्यक्त्वा मुकुन्दचरणं निरयं व्रजन्ति ॥ ११ ॥

kvedaṁ kalevaram aneka-rujāṁ nidānam
ante 'pi yasya kṛmi-bhasma-purīṣa-saṁjñāḥ |
tasmin vidhāya kudhiyo mamatām ahantāṁ
tyaktvā mukunda-caraṇaṁ nirayaṁ vrajanti || 11 ||

Word-For-Word Meanings

kva – where; *idam* – this; *kalevaram* – body; *aneka-rujām* – of innumerable torments; *nidānam* – the cause; *ante* – at the end; *api* – even; *yasya* – whose; *kṛmi-bhasma-purīṣa-saṁjñāḥ* – known as worms, ashes and excrement; *tasmin* – on which; *vidhāya* – having based; *kudhiyaḥ* – fools; *mamatām* – the concept of 'mine;' *ahantām* – the concept of 'I;' *tyaktvā* – having given up; *mukunda-caraṇam* – the lotus feet of Lord Mukunda; *nirayam* – to hell; *vrajanti* – go.

Translation

What is this body, the cause of innumerable torments, and which at the end becomes worms, ashes and excrement? Giving up the lotus feet of Lord Mukunda, fools base their concepts of 'I' and 'mine' on this body and go to hell.

TEXT 12

अहं कर्ता भोक्ता मतिरियमभूद्यस्य मम ते
स्वरूपं दुर्ज्ञेयं परमविदुषो गोकुलपते ।
स एवाद्य त्वाहं शरणमनुयातो जडमतिस्
त्वमीशोऽहं भृत्यः कुरु यदुचितं नाथ शिरसि ॥ १२ ॥

ahaṁ kartā bhoktā matir iyam abhūd yasya mama te
sva-rūpaṁ dur-jñeyaṁ parama-viduṣo gokula-pate |
sa evādya tvāhaṁ śaraṇam anuyāto jaḍa-matis
tvam īśo 'haṁ bhṛtyaḥ kuru yad ucitaṁ nātha śirasi || 12 ||

Word-For-Word Meanings

aham – I; *kartā* – doer; *bhoktā* – enjoyer; *matiḥ* – idea; *iyam* – this; *abhūt* – became; *yasya* – whose; *mama* – my; *te* – Your; *sva-rūpam* – original spiritual nature; *dur-jñeyam* – very difficult to understand; *parama-viduṣaḥ* – of the supreme wise One; *gokula-pate* – O Lord of Gokula; *saḥ* – this; *eva* – very same; *adya* – today; *tvā* – to You; *aham* – I; *śaraṇam* – shelter; *anuyātaḥ* – come; *jaḍa-matiḥ* – dull-headed; *tvam* – You; *īśaḥ* – master; *aham* – I; *bhṛtyaḥ* – servant; *kuru* – do; *yat* – whatever; *ucitam* – proper; *nātha* – O Lord; *śirasi* – on my head.

Translation

The original spiritual nature of Yours, the supreme wise Lord, is very difficult to understand for someone like me, who is absorbed in the idea of being the doer and the enjoyer. O Lord of Gokula, today this dull-headed one has taken Your shelter. You are the master and I am Your servant, so do with me whatever You deem proper, O Lord.

TEXT 13

विरिञ्चिर्ब्रह्माण्डं रचयति यदाज्ञार्पितमनाः
स्वयं विष्णुः पाति त्रिभुवनगुरोर्यस्य वशगः ।
हरत्यस्माद्भीतः कृतविकृतरूपोऽपि गिरिशस्
तमीडे ब्रह्मादित्रयनियमनं गोपतनयम् ॥ १३ ॥

viriñcir brahmāṇḍaṁ racayati yad-ājñārpita-manāḥ
svayaṁ viṣṇuḥ pāti tri-bhuvana-guror yasya vaśagaḥ |
haraty asmād bhītaḥ kṛta-vikṛta-rūpo 'pi giriśas
tam īḍe brahmādi-traya-niyamanaṁ gopa-tanayam || 13 ||

Word-For-Word Meanings

viriñciḥ – Brahmā; *brahmāṇḍam* – the universe; *racayati* – creates; *yad* – Whose; *ājñārpita-manāḥ* – whose mind is fixed on the order; *svayam* – Himself; *viṣṇuḥ* – Lord Viṣṇu; *pāti* – protects; *tri-bhuvana-guroḥ* – of the guru of the three worlds; yasya – Whose; *vaśagaḥ* – under the control; *harati* – destroys; *asmāt* – of Him; *bhītaḥ* – afraid; *kṛta-vikṛta-rūpaḥ* – whose form changes; *api* – also; *giriśaḥ* – Lord Śiva; *tam* – to Him; *īḍe* – I worship; *brahmādi-traya-niyamanam* – subduer of Brahmā, Viṣṇu and Śiva.; *gopa-tanayam* – the son of the cowherd man.

Translation

Lord Brahmā fixes his mind on His order and then creates the universe. Lord Viṣṇu Himself, Who protects the creation, is under the control of Him, the Guru of the three worlds. Even Lord Śiva changes his form and destroys the universe out of fear of Him. I worship that son of Nanda Mahārāja, Who subdues Lord Brahmā, Lord Viṣṇu and Lord Śiva.

TEXT 14

असौ मकरकेतनः कृतनिकेतनो मानसे
विलुण्ठति ममाखिलं मतिविवेकधैर्यादिकम् ।
व्रजेश जहि सत्वरं तमिममात्मपातप्रदं
न हन्तुमपरः प्रभुस्त्वमसि वीरधीराग्रणीः ॥ १४ ॥

asau makara-ketanaḥ kṛta-niketano mānase
viluṇṭhati mamākhilaṁ mati-viveka-dhairyādikam |
vrajeśa jahi satvaraṁ tam imam ātma-pāta-pradaṁ
na hantum aparaḥ prabhus tvam asi vīra-dhīrāgraṇīḥ || 14 ||

Word-For-Word Meanings

asau – that; *makara-ketanaḥ* – *Cupid; kṛta-niketanaḥ* – who made a residence; *mānase* – in the heart; *viluṇṭhati* – steals; *mama* – my; *akhilam* – all; *mati-viveka-dhairyādikam* – intelligence, discrimination, fortitude, etc.; *vrajeśa* – O Lord of Vraja; *jahi* – please kill; *satvaram* – quickly; *tam* – him; *imam* – this; *ātma-pāta-pradam* – degrader of the soul; *na* – not; *hantum* – to kill; *aparaḥ* – someone else; *prabhuḥ* – capable; *tvam* – You; *asi* – are; *vīra-dhīrāgraṇīḥ* – the bravest and strongest enemies.

Translation

Cupid has made a residence in my heart and steals all my intelligence, discrimination, fortitude, etc. O Lord of Vraja, please quickly kill this degrader of the soul. No one else can kill him, for only You are capable of killing the bravest and strongest enemies.

TEXT 15

कश्चिन्निन्दति नौति कोऽपि सुखयत्येकः परो दुःखय-
त्यन्यो गायति कोऽपि रोदिति हसत्यन्यः परः सीदति।
दत्तेऽन्यो हरते परस्वमपरो हन्त्यन्य एकोऽवति
प्रेक्ष्यैवं जगतो विनोदमनिशं त्वां कृष्णचन्द्राश्रये ॥ १५ ॥

kaścin nindati nauti ko 'pi sukhayaty ekaḥ paro duḥkhaya-
ty anyo gāyati ko 'pi roditi hasaty anyaḥ paraḥ sīdati |
datte 'nyo harate parasvam aparo hanty anya eko 'vati
prekṣyaivaṁ jagato vinodam aniśaṁ tvāṁ kṛṣṇa-candrāśraye || 15 ||

Word-For-Word Meanings

kaścit – someone; *nindati* – blames; *nauti* – praises; *kaḥ api* – someone; *sukhayati* – feels happy; *ekaḥ* – someone; *paraḥ* – another; *duḥkhayati* – feels miserable; *anyaḥ* – another; *gāyati* – sings; *kaḥ api* – someone; *roditi* – cries; *hasati* – laughs; *anyaḥ* – someone else; *paraḥ* – another; *sīdati* – is depressed; *datte* – gives donations; *anyaḥ* – someone else; *harate* – steals; *parasvam* – another's property; *aparaḥ* – someone else; *hanti* – attacks; *anyaḥ* – another; *ekaḥ* –

someone; *avati* – protects; *prekṣya* – having observed; *evam* – such; *jagataḥ* – of the world; *vinodam* – play; *aniśam* – continuous; *tvām* – to You; *kṛṣṇa-candra* – O moon-faced Kṛṣṇa; *āśraye* – I surrender.

Translation

Someone blames, someone else praises; one feels happy, another feels miserable; one person sings, another one cries, someone else laughs, and yet another is depressed; someone gives donations, someone else steals another's property; one person attacks, another protects. Having observed such continuous universal play, I surrender unto You, O moon-faced Kṛṣṇa.

TEXT 16

कति कति पितरो वा भ्रातरो मातरो वा
सुतदुहितृकलत्रभ्रातृजा बन्धवो वा।
अतिरभसकराले कालदंष्ट्रान्तराले
मम न निपतितास्ते नाथ शोचामि कं कम् ॥ १६ ॥

kati kati pitaro vā bhrātaro mātaro vā
suta-duhitṛ-kalatra-bhrātṛjā bandhavo vā |
ati-rabhasa-karāle kāla-daṁṣṭrāntarāle
mama na nipatitās te nātha śocāmi kaṁ kam || 16 ||

Word-For-Word Meanings

kati kati – how many; *pitaraḥ* – fathers; *vā* – and; *bhrātaraḥ* – brothers; *mātaraḥ* – mothers; *vā* – and; *suta-duhitṛ-kalatra-bhrātṛjāḥ* – sons, daughters, wives and nephews; *bandhavaḥ* –

friends; *vā* – and; *ati-rabhasa-karāle* – very terrible and fierce; *kāla-daṁṣṭrāntarāle* – between the teeth of death; *mama* – my; *na* – not; *nipatitāḥ* – fallen; *te* – they; *nātha* – O Lord; *śocāmi* – I lament; *kaṁ kam* – for whom.

Translation

How many fathers, mothers, sons, daughters, wives, nephews and friends did I have? Have all of them not fallen between the terrible and fierce teeth of death? O Lord, for whom should I lament?

TEXT 17

संसारारण्यगर्भे कुजनकरिघटाध्वस्तधैर्यद्रुमेऽहं
त्यक्तः पित्रा च मात्रा सुतदुहितृकलत्रादिभिर्बन्धुवर्गैः ।
हस्तं मा मुञ्च नाथ त्वमपि मम यतोऽनाथनाथोऽसि कृष्ण
क्षीणस्त्वामाश्रितोऽहं शरणदमपरं नैव पश्यामि लोके ॥ १७ ॥

saṁsārāraṇya-garbheku-jana-kari-ghaṭā-dhvasta-dhairya-drume 'haṁ
tyaktaḥ pitrā ca mātrā suta-duhitṛ-kalatrādibhir bandhu-vargaiḥ |
hastaṁ mā muñca nātha tvam api mama yato 'nātha-nātho 'si kṛṣṇa
kṣīṇas tvām āśrito 'haṁ śaraṇa-dam aparaṁ naiva paśyāmi loke || 17 ||

Word-For-Word Meanings

saṁsārāraṇya-garbhe – inside the forest of material existence; *ku-jana-kari-ghaṭā-dhvasta-dhairya-drume* – on a tree whose steadiness has been destroyed by herds of elephants in the form of wicked people; *aham* – I; *tyaktaḥ* – given up; *pitrā* – by my father; *ca* – and; *mātrā* – by my mother; *suta-duhitṛ-kalatrādibhiḥ* – by sons, daughters, wives, etc.; *bandhu-vargaiḥ* – by groups of friends; *hastam* – hand; *mā* – do not; *muñca* – release; *nātha* – O Lord; *tvam* – You; *api* – also; *mama* – my; *yataḥ* – because; *anātha-nāthaḥ* – the Lord of the helpless; *asi* – are; *kṛṣṇa* – O Kṛṣṇa; *kṣīṇaḥ* – poor; *tvām* – to You; *āśritaḥ* – surrendered; *aham* – I; *śaraṇa-dam* – giver of shelter; *aparam* – someone else; *na* – not; *eva* – indeed; *paśyāmi* – see; *loke* – in this world.

Translation

Being given up by my father, mother, sons, daughters, wife and friends inside the forest of material existence, I am on a tree whose steadiness has been destroyed by herds of elephants in the form of wicked people. O Lord, please do not release my hand like the others did, for You are the Lord of the helpless, and I am a poor soul surrendered unto You, O Kṛṣṇa. I do not see anyone else in this world who could give me shelter.

TEXT 18

सन्तापैर्विविधैः समर्दिततनुं कालो बिडालोपमो
मां प्रत्युत्कटमीक्षते निपतितं जीर्णे जगत्पञ्जरे ।
आपातालसुरालयं न भवतः पातालमन्यो जनस्
तेनाहं तव नाम गोकुलपते तिष्ठामि नित्यं जपन् ॥ १८ ॥

santāpair vividhaiḥ samardita-tanuṁ kālo biḍālopamo
māṁ praty utkaṭam īkṣate nipatitaṁ jīrṇe jagat-pañjare |
āpātāla-surālayaṁ na bhavataḥ pātālam anyo janas
tenāhaṁ tava nāma gokula-pate tiṣṭhāmi nityaṁ japan || 18 ||

Word-For-Word Meanings

santāpaiḥ – by torments; *vividhaiḥ* – manyfold; *samardita-tanum* – afflicted body; *kālaḥ* – death; *biḍālopamaḥ* – like a cat; *mām* – me; *prati* – towards; *utkaṭam* – angrily; *īkṣate* – staring at; *nipatitam* – fallen; *jīrṇe* – ancient; *jagat-pañjare* – in the cage of the material world; *āpātāla-surālayam* – from the nether world up to the heavenly planets; *na* – not; *bhavataḥ* – than You; *pātā* – protector; *alam* – able; *anyaḥ* – other; *janaḥ* – person; *tena* – therefore; *aham* – I; *tava* – Your; *nāma* – Holy Name; *gokula-pate* – O Lord of Gokula; *tiṣṭhāmi* – keep on; *nityam* – always; *japan* – chanting.

Translation

Death is like a cat staring angrily at me, my body afflicted by manifold torments, fallen into the ancient cage of this material world. From the nether world up to the heavenly planets, besides You there is no one able to protect me. O Lord of Gokula, therefore I keep on always chanting Your Holy Name.

TEXT 19

न कालिन्दी दृष्टा विमलजलकल्लोलकलिता
न वृन्दारण्याली कुसुमितलतापादपततिः।
न सन्तः सन्तोषामृतलहरिपूर्णाश्च मिलिता
मम व्यर्थं जन्म व्यगमदमलब्रह्मकुलजम् ॥ १९ ॥

na kālindī dṛṣṭā vimala-jala-kallola-kalitā
na vṛndāraṇyālī kusumita-latā-pādapa-tatiḥ |

na santaḥ santoṣāmṛta-lahari-pūrṇāś ca militā
mama vyarthaṁ janma vyagamad amala-brahma-kula-jam || 19 ||

Word-For-Word Meanings

na – not; *kālindī* – Yamunā; *dṛṣṭā* – seen; *vimala-jala-kallola-kalitā* – endowed with waves of crystal water; *na* – not; *vṛndāraṇyālī* – row of Tulasī forests; *kusumita-latā-pādapa-tatiḥ* – row of bloosomed creepers and trees; *na* – not; *santaḥ* – saintly persons; *santoṣāmṛta-lahari-pūrṇāḥ* – filled with waves of joy and nectar; *ca* – also; *militā* – met; *mama* – my; *vyartham* – in vain; *janma* – birth; *vyagamat* – spent; *amala-brahma-kula-jam* – in a pure *brāhmaṇa* family.

Translation

I have not seen the Yamunā with its waves of crystal water, or the rows of Tulasī, forest trees and blossomed creepers. Nor have I met the saintly persons who live there filled with waves of joy and nectar. In this way my birth in a pure *brāhmaṇa* family was spent in vain.

TEXT 20

हरेः पादाम्भोजे न भजनरुचिः प्रादुरभवन्
न वेदान्तज्ञानादजनि जनिहर्ताप्यनुभवः ।
न कौशल्यं कर्मण्यपि विधिनिरुक्ते पुनरभूज्
जगत्यागत्यासीत्किमिह मम कार्यं नरपशोः ॥ २० ॥

hareḥ pādāmbhoje na bhajana-ruciḥ prādurabhavan
na vedānta-jñānād ajani jani-hartāpy anubhavaḥ |

na kauśalyaṁ karmaṇy api vidhi-nirukte punar abhūj
jagaty āgatyāsīt kim iha mama kāryaṁ nara-paśoḥ || 20 ||

Word-For-Word Meanings

hareḥ – of Lord Hari; *pādāmbhoje* – the lotus feet; *na* – not; *bhajana- ruciḥ* – taste for worshipping; *prādurabhavat* – did not arise; *na* – not; *vedānta-jñānāt* – from the knowledge of Vedānta; *ajani* – was produced; *jani-hartā* – remover of birth; *api* – also; *anubhavaḥ* – realization; *na* – not; *kauśalyam* – skill; *karmaṇi* – in Vedic rituals; *api* – and; *vidhi- nirukte* – in injunctions and etymology; *punaḥ* – again; *abhūt* – there was; *jagati* – in this world; *āgatya* – having come; *āsīt* – was; *kim* – what; *iha* – here; *mama* – my; *kāryam* – activity; *nara-paśoḥ* – of a human beast.

Translation

The taste for worshipping the lotus feet of Lord Hari did not arise. Knowledge of Vedānta did not produce any realization to remove birth. I did not acquire any skill in Vedic rituals, injunctions or etymology. Having come again to this material world, what did I do here but live like a human beast?

TEXT 21

दाराः कारागृहं मे सुतदुहितृसुहृद्बान्धवः पादबन्धः
सद्मव्यापारचेष्टा लकुटशतहतिर्घातकः कर्मभारः ।
तृष्णा कृष्टिः कचानां खलजनवचनं तप्तसन्दंशतुल्यं
त्वं पाता कृष्ण नान्यो मम शरणमिह त्वां विना गोकुलेश ॥ २१ ॥

dārāḥ kārā-gṛhaṁ me suta-duhitṛ-suhṛd-bāndhavaḥ pāda-bandhaḥ
sadma-vyāpāra-ceṣṭā lakuṭa-śata-hatir ghātakaḥ karma-bhāraḥ |
tṛṣṇā kṛṣṭiḥ kacānāṁ khala-jana-vacanaṁ tapta-sandaṁśa-tulyaṁ
tvaṁ pātā kṛṣṇa nānyo mama śaraṇam iha tvāṁ vinā gokuleśa || 21 ||

Word-For-Word Meanings

dārāḥ – wife; *kārā-gṛham* – prison; *me* – my; *suta-duhitṛ-suhṛd- bāndhavaḥ* – sons, daughters, friends and relatives; *pāda-bandhaḥ* – fetters on my feet; *sadma-vyāpāra-ceṣṭā* – dealing in the market; *lakuṭa-śata-hatiḥ* – the stroke of hundreds of sticks; *ghātakaḥ* – killer; *karma- bhāraḥ* – the burden of work; *tṛṣṇā* – desire; *kṛṣṭiḥ* – dragging; *kacānām* – of elephants; *khala-jana-vacanam* – the words of wicked people; *tapta-sandaṁśa-tulyam* – like red hot pincers; *tvam* – You; *pātā* – the protector; *kṛṣṇa* – O Kṛṣṇa; *na* – not; *anyaḥ* – other; *mama* – my; *śaraṇam* – shelter; *iha* – here; *tvām* – You; *vinā* – except; *gokuleśa* – O Lord of Gokula.

Translation

My wife is like a prison; my sons, daughters, friends and relatives are like fetters on my feet; dealing in the market is like the stroke of hundreds of sticks; the burden of work is like a killer; desire is like being dragged by elephants; the words of wicked people are like red hot pincers. O Kṛṣṇa, You are my only protector. Without You I have no other shelter in this world, O Lord of Gokula.

TEXT 22

कलिना मलिनाः कृता जलौघाः
बलिना नाथ न केऽपि भोगपङ्कैः ।

अधुना मधुनायक प्रभो माम्
अवशं पातुमिह क्षमोऽसि नान्यः ॥ २२ ॥

kalinā malināḥ kṛtā jalaughāḥ
balinā nātha na ke 'pi bhoga-paṅkaiḥ |
adhunā madhu-nāyaka prabho mām
avaśaṁ pātum iha kṣamo 'si nānyaḥ || 22 ||

Word-For-Word Meanings

kalinā – by the Age of Kali; *malināḥ* – polluted; *kṛtāḥ* – made; *jalaughāḥ* – streams of water; *balinā* – strong; *nātha* – O Lord; *na* – not; *ke api* – which; *bhoga-paṅkaiḥ* – with the mud of wordly pleasures; *adhunā* – now; *madhu-nāyaka* – O sweet Lord; *prabho* – O master; *mām* – me; *avaśam* – helpless; *pātum* – to protect; *iha* – in this world; *kṣamaḥ* – able; *asi* – are; *na* – not; *anyaḥ* – other.

Translation

O Lord, who has not become polluted with worldly pleasures by the strong Age of Kali like streams of water polluted by mud? My sweet Lord, except for You, there is no one else in this world able to protect someone as helpless as me, O master.

TEXT 23

कालव्यालवृतो मदेभसहितः षड्धाटपाटच्चरो
लोभाख्येन वृकेण रुद्रगमनः क्रोधाख्यपञ्चाननः ।
ईर्ष्यामत्सरमोहकण्टकतरुछन्नो भवाध्वा हरे
लङ्घ्योऽयं कथमीश दुर्गमतरस्त्वं मे सहायं कुरु ॥ २३ ॥

kāla-vyāla-vṛto madebha-sahitaḥ ṣaḍdhāṭa-pāṭaccaro
lobhākhyena vṛkeṇa rudra-gamanaḥ krodhākhya-pañcānanaḥ |
īrṣyā-matsara-moha-kaṇṭaka-taru-channo bhavādhvā hare
laṅghyo 'yaṁ katham īśa durgamataras tvaṁ me sahāyaṁ kuru || 23 ||

Word-For-Word Meanings

kāla-vyāla-vṛtaḥ – with a snake called time; *madebha-sahitaḥ* – together with an elephant called madness; *ṣaḍdhāṭa-pāṭaccaraḥ* – six kinds of roaming thieves; *lobhākhyena* – called greed; *vṛkeṇa* – with a wolf; *rudra-gamanaḥ* – which has a fierce gait; *krodhākhya-pañcānanaḥ* – a lion called anger; *īrṣyā-matsara-moha-kaṇṭaka-taru-channaḥ* – covered with thorny bushes in the form of envy, jealousy and illusion; *bhavādhvā* – the path of material existence; *hare* – O Lord Hari; *laṅghyaḥ* – to be crossed; *ayam* – this; *katham* – how; *īśa* – O Lord; *durgamataraḥ* – impassable; *tvam* – You; *me* – me; *sahāyam* – help; *kuru* – do.

Translation

There are six thieves[1] roaming with a snake called time and an elephant called madness. A lion called anger walks fiercely with a wolf called greed. O Lord Hari, this path of material existence is covered with thorny bushes in the form of envy, jealousy and illusion. How can such an impassable path be crossed? O Lord, please help me.

TEXT 24

संसारावर्तगर्तप्रपतनभयतो नाथ ते पादमूलं
सर्वश्रेयोऽनुकूलं शरणमुपगतं पाहि मां दीनबन्धो ।

1. The five senses and the mind.

त्वामन्वञ्चो भवाध्वन्यपि दधति न ते दुर्गमे दुर्गतिं तां
यां त्वद्ध्यानप्रसङ्गच्युतमतिमिलिताम्चित्ता लभन्ते ॥ २४ ॥

saṁsārāvarta-garta-prapatana-bhayato nātha te pāda-mūlaṁ
sarva-śreyo 'nukūlaṁ śaraṇam upagataṁ pāhi māṁ dīna-bandho |
tvām anvañco bhavādhvany api dadhati na te durgame durgatiṁ tāṁ
yāṁ tvad-dhyāna-prasaṅga-cyuta-mati-militāmūla-cittā labhante || 24 ||

Word-For-Word Meanings

saṁsārāvarta-garta-prapatana-bhayataḥ – from the fear of falling into the pit of material existence; *nātha* – O Lord; *te* – Your; *pāda-mūlam* – lotus feet; *sarva-śreyaḥ* – best; *anukūlam* – favour; *śaraṇam* – shelter; *upagatam* – approached; *pāhi* – protect; *mām* – me; *dīna-bandho* – O friend of the distressed; *tvām* – You; *anvañcaḥ* – those who follow; *bhavādhvani* – on the path of material existence; *api* – although; *dadhati* – suffer; *na* – not; *te* – they; *durgame* – impassable; *durgatim* – misfortune; *tāṁ yām* – as that which; *tvad-dhyāna-prasaṅga-cyuta-mati-militāmūla-cittāḥ* – those minds are not fixed on You and whose intelligence is averse to engaging in meditating on You; *labhante* – attain.

Translation

O Lord, Your lotus feet are the best favour against the fear of falling into the pit of material existence. O friend of the distressed, please protect this surrendered soul. Although situated on this impassable path of material existence, those who follow You do not suffer the same misfortune as those whose minds are not fixed on You and whose intelligence is averse to engaging in meditating on You.

TEXT 25

अपायशतसंकुलः क्व नरकाय कायद्रुमः
क्व चेह पदमात्मनः क्व च निजाभिमानोदयः।
क्व तत्र रतिरद्भुता क्व नु विलासभोगोद्यमो
न किं किमकृत प्रभो सुहृदि पुंसि माया तव ॥ २५ ॥

apāya-śata-saṅkulaḥ kva narakāya kāya-drumaḥ
kva ceha padam ātmanaḥ kva ca nijābhimānodayaḥ |
kva tatra ratir adbhutā kva nu vilāsa-bhogodyamo
na kiṁ kim akṛta prabho suhṛdi puṁsi māyā tava || 25 ||

Word-For-Word Meanings

apāya-śata-saṅkulaḥ – perplexed by hundreds of calamities; *kva* – where; *narakāya* – for hell; *kāya-drumaḥ* – tree-like body; *kva* – where; *ca* – and; *iha* – in this world; *padam* – position; *ātmanaḥ* – of oneself; *kva* – where; *ca* – and; *nijābhimānodayaḥ* – the rising of one's pride; *kva* – where; *tatra* – there; *ratiḥ* – affection; *adbhutā* – astonishing; *kva* – where; *nu* – indeed; *vilāsa-bhogodyamaḥ* – endeavour to enjoy mundane pleasure; *na* – not; *kiṁ kim* – what; *akṛta* – done; *prabho* – O Lord; *suhṛdi* – in the heart; *puṁsi* – of a man; *māyā* – the illusory energy; *tava* – Your.

Translation

Perplexed by hundreds of calamities, this tree-like body is meant for hell. What is one's position in this world? Yet how proud one feels! How astonishing affection is! How much one endeavours to enjoy mundane pleasures! O

Lord, what has your illusory energy not done in the heart of men?

TEXT 26

क्वाहं मृगो रहसि शुष्कतृणाभिलाषी
पातः क्व मे सपदि संसृतिवागुरायाम् ।
क्व व्याधबाणकृतदुःसहमर्मपीडा
जाने परं विषयलोभमनर्थहेतुम् ॥ २६ ॥

kvāhaṁ mṛgo rahasi śuṣka-tṛṇābhilāṣī
pātaḥ kva me sapadi saṁsṛti-vāgurāyām |
kva vyādha-bāṇa-kṛta-duḥsaha-marma-pīḍā
jāne paraṁ viṣaya-lobham anartha-hetum || 26 ||

Word-For-Word Meanings

kva – where; *aham* – I; *mṛgaḥ* – deer; *rahasi* – in a desolate place; *śuṣka-tṛṇābhilāṣī* – longing for dry grass; *pātaḥ* – fallen; *kva* – where; *me* – my; *sapadi* – in a moment; *saṁsṛti-vāgurāyām* – into the trap of material existence; *kva* – where; *vyādha-bāṇa-kṛta-duḥsaha-marma-pīḍā* – the unbearable pain in my vital organs caused by the arrows of the hunter; *jāne* – I know; *param* – ultimate; *viṣaya-lobham* – greed for sense enjoyment; *anartha-hetum* – the cause for this misfortune.

Translation

Alas, like a deer longing for dry grass in a desolate place, in a moment I fell into the trap of material existence. How unbearable is the pain in my vital organs due to the arrows of the hunter! I know that the ultimate cause for this misfortune is greed for sense enjoyment.

TEXT 27

हंसः क्वाहं सरसि विमले पद्मखण्डैकवासी
क्वेदानीं मे पतनमभवत्पल्वले पङ्कपूर्णे ।
शैवालेऽस्मिंश्चरणनिगडे भग्नपक्षोऽहमासं
हंसं यातः शरणमधुना तं सखा यो ममाभूत् ॥ २७ ॥

haṁsaḥ kvāhaṁ sarasi vimale padma-khaṇḍaika-vāsī
kvedānīṁ me patanam abhavat palvale paṅka-pūrṇe |
śaivāle 'smiṁś caraṇa-nigaḍe bhagna-pakṣo 'ham āsaṁ
haṁsaṁ yātaḥ śaraṇam adhunā taṁ sakhā yo mamābhūt || 27 ||

Word-For-Word Meanings

haṁsaḥ – swan; *kva* – where; *aham* – I; *sarasi* – in the lake; *vimale* – clear; *padma-khaṇḍaika-vāsī* – living among bunches of lotuses; *kva* – where; *idānīm* – now; *me* – my; *patanam* – fall; *abhavat* – happened; *palvale* – in a tank; *paṅka-pūrṇe* – full of mud; *śaivāle* – covered with moss; *asmin* – in this; *caraṇa-nigaḍe* – the shackles on my feet; *bhagna-pakṣaḥ* –whose wings are broken; *aham* – I; *āsam* – became; *haṁsam* – to another swan; *yātaḥ* – approached; *śaraṇam* – shelter; *adhunā* – now; *tam* – him; *sakhā* – friend; *yaḥ* – who; *mama* – my; *abhūt* – became.

Translation

I was like a swan living among bunches of lotuses in a clear lake, but now I have fallen into a tank full of mud.

My feet have shackles covered with moss and my wings have become broken. I have now taken shelter of another swan, Who became my friend.

TEXT 28

संसारदुःखबृहदम्बुधिशोषणाय
वृन्दावनाख्यकलसप्रभवश्चकास्ति ।
मूढस्तथापि परितापमुपैमि सोऽहं
मोहं हरे हर कुरुष्व मयि प्रसादम् ॥ २८ ॥

saṁsāra-duḥkha-bṛhad-ambudhi-śoṣaṇāya
vṛndāvanākhya-kalasa-prabhavaś cakāsti |
mūḍhas tathāpi paritāpam upaimi so 'haṁ
mohaṁ hare hara kuruṣva mayi prasādam || 28 ||

Word-For-Word Meanings

saṁsāra-duḥkha-bṛhad-ambudhi-śoṣaṇāya – for drying the great ocean of the misery of material existence; *vṛndāvanākhya-kalasa-prabhavaḥ* – a second Agastya Muni called Vṛndāvana; *cakāsti* – shines forth; *mūḍhaḥ* – fool; *tathā api* – still; *paritāpam* – tribulation; *upaimi* – undergo; *saḥ* – this; *aham* – I; *moham* – illusion; *hare* – O Lord Hari; *hara* – remove; *kuruṣva* – do; *mayi* – upon me; *prasādam* – mercy.

Translation

To dry up the great ocean of the misery of material existence, a second Agastya Muni called Vṛndāvana shines forth.[2] Still, this fool is just undergoing tribulations somewhere else. O Lord Hari, please remove my illusion and give me Your mercy.

TEXT 29

तावत्कामो विकटकुटिलप्रेक्षणैरीक्षतां मां
क्रोधाग्नेर्वा हृदयसदनं विस्फुलिङ्गा दहन्तु ।
लोभव्याघ्रोऽप्यहह परितः सृक्किणीं लेढु गाढं
यावद् वृन्दाविपिनधरणी न प्रयात्यक्षिमार्गम् ॥ २९ ॥

tāvat kāmo vikaṭa-kuṭila-prekṣaṇair īkṣatāṁ māṁ
krodhāgner vā hṛdaya-sadanaṁ visphuliṅgā dahantu |
lobha-vyāghro 'py ahaha paritaḥ sṛkviṇīṁ leḍhu gāḍhaṁ
yāvad vṛndā-vipina-dharaṇī na prayāty akṣi-mārgam || 29 ||

Word-For-Word Meanings

tāvat – so long; *kāmaḥ* – lust; *vikaṭa-kuṭila-prekṣaṇaiḥ* – with hideous crooked glances; *īkṣatām* – may stare; *mām* – me; *krodhāgneḥ* – of the fire of anger; *vā* – and; *hṛdaya-sadanam* – the seat of the heart; *visphuliṅgāḥ* – sparks; *dahantu* – may burn; *lobha-vyāghraḥ* – the tiger of greed; *api* – and; *ahaha* – ah; *paritaḥ* – around; *sṛkviṇīm* – corner of the mouth; *leḍhu* – may lick; *gāḍham* – avidly; *yāvat* – as long as; *vṛndā-vipina- dharaṇī* – the land of Vṛndāvana; *na* – not; *prayāti* – comes; *akṣi- mārgam* – before my eyes.

---

2. The *Mahābhārata* (Vana-parva, chapters 100-104) narrates how Agastya Muni, who was born from a pitcher (*kalasa-prabhavaḥ*), swallowed the ocean. Here the author glorifies the sanctity of Vṛndāvana by comparing it with Agastya Muni, for it is able to make the whole ocean of miseries dry.

Translation

As long as the land of Vṛndāvana does not come before my eyes, let lust stare at me with hideous crooked glances and let the sparks of the fire of anger burn my chest. Ah, let the tiger of greed avidly lick the corner of its mouth.

TEXT 30

तावन्मोहमहाहिरुग्रगरलव्यालोलदृग्वीक्षताम्
आधिव्याधिशतप्रमत्तकरटिव्याटोप उज्जृम्भताम् ।
वर्धन्तामनिशं जरामरणभीशोकद्रुमा दुःसहा
यावत्कर्णपथं न याति यमुनाकल्लोलकोलाहलः ॥ ३० ॥

tāvan moha-mahāhir ugra-garala-vyālola-dṛg vīkṣatām
ādhi-vyādhi-śata-pramatta-karaṭi-vyāṭopa ujjṛmbhatām |
vardhantām aniśaṁ jarā-maraṇa-bhī-śoka-drumā duḥsahā
yāvat karṇa-pathaṁ na yāti yamunā-kallola-kolāhalaḥ || 30 ||

Word-For-Word Meanings

tāvat – so long; *moha-mahāhiḥ* – the great snake of illusion; *ugra-garala-vyālola-dṛk* – with eyes rolling due to its fierce poison; *vīkṣatām* – may stare; *ādhi-vyādhi-śata-pramatta-karaṭi-vyāṭopaḥ* – the mad elephant of pride with hundreds of miseries and ailments; *ujjṛmbhatām* – may come forth; *vardhantām* – may grow; *aniśam* – continuously; *jarā-maraṇa-bhī-śoka-drumāḥ* – the trees of grief, fear, old age and death; *duḥsahāḥ* – unbearable; *yāvat* – as long as; *karṇa-patham* – the scope of the ears; *na* – not; *yāti* – reach; *yamunā-kallola-kolāhalaḥ* – the sound of the waves of the Yamunā.

Translation

As long as the sound of the waves of the Yamunā does not reach my ears, let the great snake of illusion stare at me with eyes rolling due to its fierce poison. Let the mad elephant of pride come forth with hundreds of miseries and ailments. Let the unbearable trees of grief, fear, old age and death grow continuously.

TEXT 31

कालव्यालविषाग्निगारुडमणिस्तापत्रयेभाङ्कुशः
श्रीविद्याकुलगर्वपर्वतपविर्दैन्यक्षपाटार्कभा ।
मोहाम्भोदघटाविनाशनशरज्जागर्ति वृन्दावनं
सीदामः करिशावका इव वृथा सूत्रेण बद्धा वयम् ॥ ३१ ॥

kāla-vyāla-viṣāgni-gāruḍa-maṇis tāpa-trayebhāṅkuśaḥ
śrī-vidyā-kula-garva-parvata-pavir dainya-kṣapāṭārkabhā |
mohāmbhoda-ghaṭā-vināśana-śaraj jāgarti vṛndāvanaṁ
sīdāmaḥ kari-śāvakā iva vṛthā sūtreṇa baddhā vayam || 31 ||

Word-For-Word Meanings

kāla-vyāla-viṣāgni-gāruḍa-maṇiḥ – an emerald against the burning poison of the snake of time; *tāpa-trayebhāṅkuśaḥ* – a goad to curb the elephant of threefold misery; *śrī-vidyā-kula-garva-parvata-paviḥ* – a thunderbolt to strike the mountain of pride due to high lineage, knowledge and beauty; *dainya-kṣapāṭārkabhā* – like a sun dispelling the fiend of distress; *mohāmbhoda-ghaṭā-vināśana-śarat* – the autumn to dissipate the assemblage of the clouds of illusion; *jāgarti* – rises; *vṛndāvanam* – Vṛndāvana; *sīdāmaḥ* –

we are sitting; *kari-śāvakāḥ* – elephant cubs; *iva* – like; *vṛthā* – in vain; *sūtreṇa* – with a rope; *baddhāḥ* – bound; *vayam* – we.

Translation

Vṛndāvana rises like a sun dispelling the fiend of distress, like an emerald[3] against the burning poison of the snake of time, like a goad to curb the elephant of threefold misery, like a thunderbolt to strike the mountain of pride due to high lineage, knowledge and beauty, like the autumn to dissipate the assemblage of the clouds of illusion. We are sitting here in vain, bound by a rope just like elephant cubs.

TEXT 32

न राज्यं नो कोशो न करटिघता नैव तुरगा
न सेना सम्पत्तिर्न च भुजबलं नैव सुमतिः ।
न विद्या नोपाया न च धनुरसिर्नैव न शरा
हरेर्नामैवास्ते शमनभयभीतस्य शरणम् ॥ ३२ ॥

na rājyaṁ no kośo na karaṭi-ghatā naiva turagā
na senā sampattir na ca bhuja-balaṁ naiva sumatiḥ |
na vidyā nopāyā na ca dhanur asir naiva na śarā
harer nāmaivāste śamana-bhaya-bhītasya śaraṇam || 32 ||

Word-For-Word Meanings

na – not; *rājyam* – kingdom; *na u* – nor; *kośaḥ* – treasury;

3. Emeralds are traditionally said to be effective against snake bite.

na – nor; *karaṭi-ghaṭāḥ* – herds of elephants; *na* – nor; *eva* – indeed; *turagāḥ* – horses; *na* – nor; *senā* – an army; *sampattiḥ* – affluence; *na* – nor; *ca* – and; *bhuja-balam* – the strength of the arms; *na* – nor; *eva* – indeed; *sumatiḥ* – intelligence; *na* – nor; *vidyā* – scholarship; *na* – nor; *upāyāḥ* – stratagems; *na* – nor; *ca* – and; *dhanuḥ* – bow; *asiḥ* – sword; *na* – nor; *eva* – indeed; *na* – nor; *śarāḥ* – arrows; *hareḥ* – of Lord Hari; *nāma* – the Holy Name; *eva* – only; *āste* – is; *śamana-bhaya-bhītasya* – for one affraid of death; *śaraṇam* – shelter.

Translation

Neither a kingdom, nor a treasury, nor herds of elephants, nor horses, nor an army, nor affluence, nor the strength of the arms, nor a good brain, nor scholarship, nor stratagems, nor bows, swords or arrows – the Holy Name of Lord Hari is the only shelter for one afraid of death.

TEXT 33

न शम्भुर्नो शक्रो न च गणपतिर्नैव वरुणो
न मार्तण्डो नेन्दुर्न कमलजनिर्नैव धनदः ।
न सिद्धा नो यज्ञा न च हुतवहो नैव मरुतो
हरिस्त्राता कण्ठार्पितशमनपाशोत्कटभयात् ॥ ३३॥

na śambhur no śakro na ca gaṇapatir naiva varuṇo
na mārtaṇḍo nendur na kamala-janir naiva dhanadaḥ |
na siddhā no yajñā na ca hutavaho naiva maruto
haris trātā kaṇṭhārpita-śamana-pāśotkaṭa-bhayāt || 33 ||

Word-For-Word Meanings

na – not; *śambhuḥ* – Śiva; *na u* – nor; *śakraḥ* – Indra; *na* – nor; *ca* – and; *gaṇapatiḥ* – Gaṇeśa; *na* – nor; *eva* – indeed; *varuṇaḥ* – Varuṇa; *na* – nor; *mārtaṇḍaḥ* – Sūrya; *na* - nor; *induḥ* – Candra; *na* – nor; *kamala-janiḥ* – Brahmā; *na* – nor; *eva* – indeed; *dhanadaḥ* – Kuvera; *na* – nor; *siddhāḥ* – the Siddhas; *na u* – nor; *yajñāḥ* – sacrificial gods; *na* – nor; *ca* – and; *hutavahaḥ* – Agni; *na* – nor; *eva* – indeed; *marutaḥ* – Vāyu; *hariḥ* – Lord Hari; *trātā* – the protector; *kaṇṭhārpita-śamana- pāśotkaṭa-bhayāt* – from the great fear of the shackles of death tightened around the neck.

Translation

Neither Śiva, nor Indra, nor Gaṇeśa, nor Varuṇa, nor Sūrya, nor Candra, nor Brahmā, nor Kuvera, nor the Siddhas, nor the sacrificial gods, nor Agni, nor Vāyu – only Lord Hari can protect from the great fear of the shackles of death tightened around the neck.

TEXT 34

न रूपं ते दृष्टं शिरसि शिखिपिच्छं रचयतो
न वंशीनादस्ते श्रवणमगमन्नाथ मधुरः ।
जनुर्जातं व्यर्थं विषमविषयाक्रान्तमनसं
कियानर्थो मेऽभूद्भवदनुगपादावभजतः ॥ ३४ ॥

na rūpaṁ te dṛṣṭaṁ śirasi śikhi-picchaṁ racayato
na vaṁśī-nādas te śravaṇam agaman nātha madhuraḥ |
janur jātaṁ vyarthaṁ viṣama-viṣayākrānta-manasaṁ
kiyān artho me 'bhūd bhavad-anuga-pādāv abhajataḥ || 34 ||

Word-For-Word Meanings

na – not; *rūpam* – form; *te* – Your; *dṛṣṭam* – seen; *śirasi* – on the head; *śikhi-piccham* – a peacock feather; *racayataḥ* – decorating; *na* – nor; *vaṁśī-nādaḥ* – the sound of the flute; *te* – Your; *śravaṇam* – hearing; *agamat* – came; *nātha* – O Lord; *madhuraḥ* – sweet; *januḥ* – birth; *jātam* – became; *vyartham* – useless; *viṣama-viṣayākrānta-manasam* – the mind being overcome by strong sense objects; *kiyāt* – how much; *arthaḥ* – gain; *me* – my; *abhūt* – became; *bhavad-anuga-pādau* – the feet of Your servants; *abhajataḥ* – not worshipping.

Translation

I did not see Your beautiful form and the peacock feather decorating Your head, nor did I hear the sweet sound of Your flute, O Lord. My mind being overcome by strong sense objects, this birth has been useless. Without worshipping the feet of Your servants, what have I gained?

TEXT 35

अहं दाता शूरो बुध इति भवान् किं मम पुरो
मिथःस्पर्धासूयाभिमतिकुमतिग्रस्तमखिलम् ।
न मूढोऽयं वेद क्व पवनवशोत्कम्पनलिनी-
दलव्यग्रं विश्वं भगवदनुवृत्तिः क्व सुखदा ॥ ३५ ॥

ahaṁ dātā śūro budha iti bhavān kiṁ mama puro
mithaḥ-spardhāsūyābhimati-kumati-grastam akhilam |
na mūḍho 'yaṁ veda kva pavana-vaśotkampa-nalinī-
dala-vyagraṁ viśvaṁ bhagavad-anuvṛttiḥ kva sukha-dā || 35 ||

Word-For-Word Meanings

aham – I; *dātā* – a donor; *śūraḥ* – a hero; *budhaḥ* – a wise man; *iti* – thus; *bhavān* – you; *kim* – what; *mama* – my; *puraḥ* – in the presence; *mithaḥ-spardhāsūyābhimati-kumati-grastam* – seized by dullness, pride, envy and rivalry towards others; *akhilam* – fully; *na* – not; *mūḍhaḥ* – fool; *ayam* – this; *veda* – knows; *kva* – where; *pavana-vaśotkampa-nalinī-dala- vyagram* – unsteady like a lotus petal shaking under the control of the wind; *viśvam* – this world; *bhagavad-anuvṛttiḥ* – service to the Supreme Lord; *kva* – where; *sukha-dā* – giving happiness.

Translation

"I am a donor, a hero and a wise man. Who are you before me?" – This fool used to behave in this way without knowing that I was fully seized by dullness, pride, envy and rivalry towards others. What is this world compared to the happiness of serving the Supreme Lord? It is unsteady just like a lotus petal shaking under the control of the wind.

TEXT 36

कियन्तो ब्रह्माणः कति कति न जाता बलभिदो
दशास्यस्वर्णाक्षप्रभृतिदनुजेन्द्रा न चलिताः ।
तथापि प्रेमाणं विदधति शरीरे कुमतयो
विहाय श्रीवृन्दावननवनिकुञ्जेशभजनम् ॥ ३६ ॥

kiyanto brahmāṇaḥ kati kati na jātā bala-bhido
daśāsya-svarṇākṣa-prabhṛti-danujendrā na calitāḥ |

tathāpi premāṇaṁ vidadhati śarīre kumatayo
vihāya śrī-vṛndāvana-nava-nikuñjeśa-bhajanam || 36 ||

Word-For-Word Meanings

kiyantaḥ – how many; *brahmāṇaḥ* – Brahmās; *kati kati* – how many; *na* – not; *jātāḥ* – born; *bala-bhidaḥ* – having their power crushed; *daśāsya-svarṇākṣa-prabhṛti-danujendrāḥ* – demoniac kings like Rāvaṇa, Hiraṇyākṣa, etc.; *na* – not; *calitāḥ* – gone; *tathā api* – still; *premāṇam* – love; *vidadhati* – give; *śarīre* – on this body; *kumatayaḥ* – foolish people; *vihāya* – having given up; *śrī-vṛndāvana-nava-nikuñjeśa-bhajanam* – the worship of the Lord of the fresh bowers of Śrī Vṛndāvana.

Translation

How many Brahmās have been born? How many demoniac kings like Rāvaṇa and Hiraṇyākṣa have gone, their power crushed into pieces? Still foolish people love this body so much and give up the worship of the Lord of the fresh bowers of Śrī Vṛndāvana.

TEXT 37

क्वेदानीं नहुषो हिरण्यकशिपुः क्वास्ति क्व वा रावणो
वेणः क्व क्व धरासुतः क्व यवनः क्वासौ सहस्रार्जुनः ।
दृश्यन्ते खलु गर्वपर्वतसमारूढाः पतन्तो जनास्
तस्मात्त्वां शरणं गतोऽस्मि भगवन् मां पाहि संसारतः ॥ ३७ ॥

kvedānīṁ nahuṣo hiraṇyakaśipuḥ kvāsti kva vā rāvaṇo
veṇaḥ kva kva dharāsutaḥ kva yavanaḥ kvāsau sahasrārjunaḥ |

dṛśyante khalu garva-parvata-samārūḍhāḥ patanto janās
tasmāt tvāṁ śaraṇaṁ gato 'smi bhagavan māṁ pāhi saṁsārataḥ || 37 ||

Word-For-Word Meanings

kva – where; *idānīm* – now; *nahuṣaḥ* – Nahuṣa; *hiraṇyakaśipuḥ* – Hiraṇyakaśipu; *kva* – where; *asti* – is; *kva* – where; *vā* – and; *rāvaṇaḥ* – Rāvaṇa; *veṇaḥ* – Veṇa; *kva* – where; *kva* – where; *dharāsutaḥ* – Bhaumāsura; *kva* – where; *yavanaḥ* – Kālayavana; *kva* – where; *asau* – that; *sahasrārjunaḥ* – Kārtavīryārjuna; *dṛśyante* – are seen; *khalu* – certainly; *garva-parvata-samārūḍhāḥ* – who climbed the mountain of pride; *patantaḥ* – falling; *janāḥ* – people; *tasmāt* – therefore; *tvām* – to You; *śaraṇam* – shelter; *gataḥ* – resorted to; *asmi* – I am; *bhagavan* – O Supreme Lord; *mām* – me; *pāhi* – protect; *saṁsārataḥ* – from the cycle of material life.

Translation

Where is Nahuṣa now? Where is Hiraṇyakaśipu? Where is Rāvaṇa? Where is Veṇa? Where is Bhaumāsura? Where is Kālayavana? Where is Kārtavīryārjuna? After climbing the mountain of pride, people are certainly seen falling down from it. Therefore I have taken shelter of You, O Lord. Please protect me from the cycle of material life.

TEXT 38

भ्रंश्यत्कुड्यपलं जराघुणकृमिध्वस्तास्थिविष्टम्भक-
स्तम्भं नश्वरधातुबन्धनमतित्रुट्यत्त्वगाच्छादनम् ।

रुद्धद्वारमिदं शरीरसदनं जीर्णं पतद्वर्तते
मूढोऽहं न तथापि शोकशमनं गच्छामि वृन्दावनम् ॥ ३८ ॥

bhraṁśyat-kuḍya-palaṁ jarā-ghuṇa-kṛmi-dhvastāsthi-viṣṭambhaka-
stambhaṁ naśvara-dhātu-bandhanam ati-truṭyat-tvag-ācchādanam |
ruddha-dvāram idaṁ śarīra-sadanaṁ jīrṇaṁ patad vartate
mūḍho 'haṁ na tathāpi śoka-śamanaṁ gacchāmi vṛndāvanam || 38 ||

Word-For-Word Meanings

bhraṁśyat-kuḍya-palam – whose walls of flesh are collapsing; *jarā-ghuṇa-kṛmi-dhvastāsthi-viṣṭambhaka-stambham* – whose supporting pillars of bones were destroyed by worms and decrepitude; *naśvara-dhātu-bandhanam* – whose construction is made of perishable elements; *ati-truṭyat-tvag-ācchādanam* – whose covering of skin is splitting; *ruddha-dvāram* – whose gates are obstructed; *idam* – this; *śarīra-sadanam* – house-like body; *jīrṇam* – old; *patat* – falling apart; *vartate* – is; *mūḍhaḥ* – fool; *aham* – I; *na* – not; *tathā api* – still; *śoka-śamanam* – which appeases distress; *gacchāmi* – go; *vṛndāvanam* – to Vṛndāvana.

Translation

This house-like body is now too old and falling apart with its gates obstructed, its walls of flesh collapsing, its supporting pillars of bones destroyed by worms and decrepitude, its covering of splitting skin, and its construction made of perishable elements. Still I am such a fool that I do not go to Vṛndāvana, which appeases distress.

TEXT 39

एतां मे तनुमेजयन्तु सततं दुःखप्रचण्डानिला
भीमोऽयं परितः प्रसर्पतु महासंसारदावानलः ।
शङ्कामङ्कुरयन्तु शोकनिवहाः किं तैर्यतः साम्प्रतं
कालिन्दीकलिकालकोपहरिणी जागर्ति भूमीतले ॥ ३९ ॥

etāṁ me tanum ejayantu satataṁ duḥkha-pracaṇḍānilā
bhīmo 'yaṁ paritaḥ prasarpatu mahā-saṁsāra-dāvānalaḥ |
śaṅkām aṅkurayantu śoka-nivahāḥ kiṁ tair yataḥ sāmprataṁ
kālindī kali-kāla-kopa-hariṇī jāgarti bhūmī-tale || 39 ||

Word-For-Word Meanings

etām – this; *me* – my; *tanum* – body; *ejayantu* – may shake; *satatam* – constantly; *duḥkha-pracaṇḍānilāḥ* – the winds of distress; *bhīmaḥ* – formidable; *ayam* – this; *paritaḥ* – in all directions; *prasarpatu* – may spread; *mahā-saṁsāra-dāvānalaḥ* – the forest fire of this great cycle of material existence; *śaṅkām* – misgiving; *aṅkurayantu* – may sprout; *śoka-nivahāḥ* – the winds of lamentation; *kiṁ taiḥ* – what matters; *yataḥ* – since; *sāmpratam* – now; *kālindī* – Yamunā; *kali-kāla-kopa-hariṇī* – who removes the anger of the Age of Kali; *jāgarti* – has appeared; *bhūmī-tale* – on earth.

Translation

Let the terrible winds of distress constantly shake my body. Let the formidable forest fire of this great cycle of material existence spread itself in all directions. Let the winds of lamentation sprout misgiving. Who cares for all of these when the river Yamunā has now appeared on earth to remove all anger in this age of Kali?

TEXT 40

जनुर्लाभः कोऽयं जगति जगदानन्दचरितो
व्रजेशो नासेवि प्रतिघटि यदि प्राणदयितः ।
भजन्तो दृश्यन्ते तमिह भवतापोत्कटशिखि-
स्फुरज्ज्वालादुःखैः सततमपरिस्पृष्टतनवः ॥ ४० ॥

janur-lābhaḥ ko 'yaṁ jagati jagad-ānanda-carito
vrajeśo nāsevi pratighaṭi yadi prāṇa-dayitaḥ |
bhajanto dṛśyante tam iha bhava-tāpotkaṭa-śikhi-
sphura-jvālā-duḥkhaiḥ satatam aparispṛṣṭa-tanavaḥ || 40 ||

Word-For-Word Meanings

janur-lābhaḥ – the advantage of birth; *kaḥ* – what; *ayam* – this; *jagati* – in this world; *jagad-ānanda-caritaḥ* – Whose transcendental activities bring joy to the whole universe; *vrajeśaḥ* – the Lord of Vraja; *na* – not; *asevi* – served; *pratighaṭi* – at every moment; *yadi* – if; *prāṇa-dayitaḥ* – giver of life; *bhajantaḥ* – worshipping; *dṛśyante* – are seen; *tam* – Him; *iha* – in this world; *bhava-tāpotkaṭa-śikhi-sphura-jvālā-duḥkhaiḥ* – by the suffering produced by the flames of the fierce fire of the miseries of material existence; *satatam* – constantly; *aparispṛṣṭa-tanavaḥ* – whose bodies are not touched.

Translation

What is the advantage of being born in this world if one does not serve the Lord of Vraja at every moment, Who is the life-giver and Whose transcendental activities bring joy to the whole universe? The bodies of those who constantly worship Him in this world are not touched by the suffering produced by the flames of the fierce fire of the miseries of material existence.

TEXT 41

मेदोमांसास्थिमज्ञाकफरुधिरवसाशुक्रविण्मूत्रपूय-
क्लेदागारं शरीरं बहिरतिविततैश्चर्मभिर्नद्धमेतत् ।
तत्किं यन्नास्ति बीभत्सितमिह तदपि स्वत्वमस्मिन् विधत्ते
लोकोऽयं मन्दबुद्धिर्न भजति चरणौ नाथ ते किं विधेयम् ॥ ४१ ॥

medo-māṁsāsthi-majjā-kapha-rudhira-vasā-śukra-viṇ-mūtra-pūya-
kledāgāraṁ śarīraṁ bahir ati-vitataiś carmabhir naddham etat |
tat kiṁ yan nāsti bībhatsitam iha tad api svatvam asmin vidhatte
loko 'yaṁ manda-buddhir na bhajati caraṇau nātha te kiṁ vidheyam ||41||

Word-For-Word Meanings

medo- māṁsāsthi- majjā- kapha- rudhira- vasā- śukra- viṇ- mūtra- pūya-kledāgāram – a house of suffering made of fat, flesh, bones, marrow, mucus, blood, semen, excrement, urine and pus; *śarīram* – body; *bahiḥ* – externally; *ati-vitataiḥ* – very long; *carmabhiḥ* – by skin; *naddham* – joined together; *etat* – this; *tat* – that; *kim* – what; *yat* – which; *na* – not; *asti* – is; *bībhatsitam* – disgusting; *iha* – here; *tat api* – yet; *svatvam* – the very self; *asmin* – in this; *vidhatte* – make; *lokaḥ* – people; *ayam* – this; *manda-buddhiḥ* – foolish; *na* – not; *bhajati* – worship; *caraṇau* – lotus feet; *nātha* – O Lord; *te* – Your; *kim* – what; *vidheyam* – should be done.

Translation

This body is a house of suffering made of fat, flesh, bones, marrow, mucus, blood, semen, excrement, urine and pus joined together and externally covered by very long skin. Is there anything here which is not disgusting? Yet foolish people consider these as their very self and do not worship Your lotus feet, O Lord. What to do?

TEXT 42

जीवा एव गजा गभीरगहनं गेहोदरं गर्तवत्
पिण्डग्रासमिव ग्रसन्ति विषयान् कर्मैव तद्बन्धनम् ।
योषाश्रृङ्खलिकेव देव सुदृढा तन्मोचनं त्वत्करे
गर्तं पूरय कर्म वारय हरे तां श्रृङ्खलां छेदय ॥ ४२ ॥

jīvā eva gajā gabhīra-gahanaṁ gehodaraṁ gartavat
piṇḍa-grāsam iva grasanti viṣayān karmaiva tad-bandhanam |
yoṣā-śṛṅkhalikeva deva sudṛḍhā tan-mocanaṁ tvat-kare
gartaṁ pūraya karma vāraya hare tāṁ śṛṅkhalāṁ chedaya || 42 ||

Word-For-Word Meanings

jīvāḥ – the conditioned souls; *eva* – indeed; *gajāḥ* – elephants; *gabhīra-gahanam* – deep and inaccessible; *gehodaram* – inside their homes; *gartavat* – like a pit; *piṇḍa-grāsam* – morsel of food; *iva* – like; *grasanti* – eating; *viṣayān* – sensual pleasures; *karma* – material activities; *eva* – only; *tad-bandhanam* – their bondage; *yoṣā-śṛṅkhalikā* – a woman's chain; *iva* – like; *deva* – O God; *sudṛḍhā* – very tight; *tan-mocanam* – their release; *tvat-kare* – in Your hand; *gartam* – the pit; *pūraya* – fill;

karma – material activities; *vāraya* – check; *hare* – O Lord Hari; *tām* – it; *śṛṅkhalām* – chain; *chedaya* – break.

Translation

The conditioned souls enjoying sensual pleasures inside their homes are like elephants eating morsels of food in a deep and inaccessible pit. Material activities are the only cause of their bondage, which is tight like a woman's chain, and their release is in Your hands, O Lord. Please fill the pit, check the material activities and break the chain, O Hari.

TEXT 43

यावज्जीवं दधति सुधियः प्रेमभावं मुकुन्दे
कालज्वालाकुलितमभितः प्रेक्ष्य पद्मासनान्तम् ।
जाता राधारमणचरणोपासनावासना चेत्
तर्ह्येव स्याद्यमकृतमहायातनापातनाशः ॥ ४३ ॥

yāvaj-jīvaṁ dadhati sudhiyaḥ prema-bhāvaṁ mukunde
kāla-jvālākulitam abhitaḥ prekṣya padmāsanāntam |
jātā rādhā-ramaṇa-caraṇopāsanā-vāsanā cet
tarhy eva syād yama-kṛta-mahā-yātanā-pāta-nāśaḥ || 43 ||

Word-For-Word Meanings

yāvaj-jīvam – as long as one lives; *dadhati* – give; *su-dhiyaḥ* – intelligent people; *prema-bhāvam* – feeling of love; *mukunde* – to Lord Mukunda; *kāla-jvālākulitam* – afflicted by the influence of blazing death; *abhitaḥ* – on all sides; *prekṣya* – having observed; *padmāsanāntam* – up to Brahmā;

jātā – arisen; *rādhā-ramaṇa-caraṇopāsanā-vāsanā* – the desire to worship the feet of Rādhā-Ramaṇa; *cet* – if; *tarhi* – then; *eva* – only; *syāt* – there would be; *yama-kṛta-mahā-yātanā-pāta-nāśaḥ* – no more falling into the severe punishment inflicted by Yamarāja.

Translation

Having observed on all sides that even up to Lord Brahmā everyone is afflicted by the influence of blazing death, intelligent people give their love to Lord Mukunda as long as they live. If one acquires the desire to worship the feet of Rādhā-Ramaṇa, then only is there no more danger of falling into the severe punishment inflicted by Yamarāja.

TEXT 44

तावन्माया नटी मे शिरसि पटुनटत्पादघातं विधत्तां
तावत्संसारदुःखानलवहनशिखाश्रेणयो भीषयन्तु ।
तावद्भोगेन सिक्ता विषयविषलता पल्लवं सम्प्रसूताम्
आकर्ण्यन्ते न यावद्दिनमणिदुहितुर्लोलकल्लोलनादाः ॥ ४४ ॥

tāvan māyā naṭī me śirasi paṭu-naṭat-pāda-ghātaṁ vidhattāṁ
tāvat saṁsāra-duḥkhānala-vahana-śikhā-śreṇayo bhīṣayantu |
tāvad bhogena siktā viṣaya-viṣa-latā pallavaṁ samprasūtām
ākarṇyante na yāvad dina-maṇi-duhitur lola-kallola-nādāḥ || 44 ||

Word-For-Word Meanings

tāvat – so long; *māyā* – the illusory energy; *naṭī* – dancer; *me* – my; *śirasi* – on the head; *paṭu-naṭat-pāda-ghātam* – strike with the feet while skilfully dancing; *vidhattām* –

may do; *tāvat* – so long; *saṁsāra-duḥkhānala-vahana-śikhā-śreṇayaḥ* – the rows of flames carrying the fire of material miseries; *bhīṣayantu* – may frighten; *tāvat* – so long; *bhogena* – with material enjoyment; *siktā* – sprinkled; *viṣaya-viṣa-latā* – the poisonous creeper of sense objects; *pallavam* – blossom; *samprasūtām* – may bring forth; *ākarṇyante* – are heard; *na* – not; *yāvat* – as long as; *dina-maṇi-duhituḥ* – of the daugher of the sungod; *lola-kallola-nādāḥ* – the sound of the rolling waves.

Translation

As long as I do not hear the sound of the rolling waves of the river Yamunā, the daughter of the sun god, so long let the dancer-like *māyā* strike my head with her feet while skilfully dancing, let the rows of flames carrying the fire of material miseries frighten me, and let the poisonous creeper of sense objects blossom, being sprinkled with material enjoyment.

TEXT 45

इयं भग्ना भित्तिश्छदिरपि गृहं जीर्णमभवत्
क्व तिष्ठेयुर्दाराः परिणयनयोग्योऽस्ति तनयः ।
गतः कालो भूयानिति विमृशतो मन्दमनसो
न लब्धा श्रीराधारमणपदसेवारतिरपि ॥ ४५ ॥

iyaṁ bhagnā bhittiś chadir api gṛhaṁ jīrṇam abhavat
kva tiṣṭheyur dārāḥ pariṇayana-yogyo 'sti tanayaḥ |
gataḥ kālo bhūyān iti vimṛśato manda-manaso
na labdhā śrī-rādhā-ramaṇa-pada-sevā-ratir api || 45 ||

Word-For-Word Meanings

iyam – this; *bhagnā* – broken; *bhittiḥ* – wall; *chadiḥ* – roof; *api* – and; *gṛham* – the house; *jīrṇam* – old; *abhavat* – became; *kva* – where; *tiṣṭheyuḥ* – would stay; *dārāḥ* – wife; *pariṇayana-yogyaḥ* – fit for marriage; *asti* – is; *tanayaḥ* – son; *gataḥ* – passed; *kālaḥ* – time; *bhūyān* – very long; *iti* – thus; *vimṛśataḥ* – pondering over; *manda-manasaḥ* – whose intelligence is slow; *na* – not; *labdhā* – attained; *śrī-rādhā-ramaṇa-pada-sevā-ratiḥ* – attachment for serving the lotus feet of Śrī-Rādhā-Ramaṇa; *api* – and.

Translation

"This wall is broken, the roof too, and the house has become too old. Where will my wife stay? My son is already of marriageable age." – A long time has passed while I was pondering over these things, dull-headed as I am, and in this way I have not developed attachment for serving the lotus feet of Śrī-Rādhā-Ramaṇa.

TEXT 46

धृता नानायोनीरिह विषयभोगोऽपि विहितो
मया मानामानौ विधिवशकृतावप्यधिगतौ ।
जनुर्नारं लब्धं तदपि गृहकृत्येन कुधिया
वृथा नीतं गीतं व्रजपतियशो नैव विमलम् ॥ ४६ ॥

dhṛtā nānā-yonīr iha viṣaya-bhogo 'pi vihito
mayā mānāmānau vidhi-vaśa-kṛtāv apy adhigatau |
janur nāraṁ labdhaṁ tad api gṛha-kṛtyena kudhiyā
vṛthā nītaṁ gītaṁ vraja-pati-yaśo naiva vimalam || 46 ||

Word-For-Word Meanings

dhṛtā – taken; *nānā-yoniḥ* – many species of life; *iha* – in this world; *viṣaya-bhogaḥ* – sense gratification; *api* – and; *vihitaḥ* – done; *mayā* – by me; *mānāmānau* – honour and dishonour; *vidhi-vaśa-kṛtau* – impelled by destiny; *api* – and; *adhigatau* – obtained; *januḥ* – birth; *nāram* – human; *labdham* – obtained; *tat api* – yet; *gṛha-kṛtyena* – with household affairs; *kudhiyā* – by this fool; *vṛthā* – in vain; *nītam* – spent; *gītam* – sung; *vraja-pati-yaśaḥ* – the glories of the Lord of Vraja; *na* – not; *eva* – indeed; *vimalam* – pure.

Translation

I have accepted birth in many species of life in this world and enjoyed sense gratification. Impelled by destiny, I obtained both honour and dishonour. Although I obtained this human birth, I have foolishly wasted it being engaged in household affairs without singing the pure glories of the Lord of Vraja.

TEXT 47

अविश्रान्तं सेवा क्षितिपतिगृहद्वारि मनुजैः
क्रियेतानर्थज्ञैर्विटनटकुटुम्बोदरकृते ।
व्रजाधीशद्वारि क्षणमपि न तिष्ठेयुरनघा
यतः सम्पत्पूर्णा हसति शतमन्योरपि पदम् ॥ ४७ ॥

aviśrāntaṁ sevā kṣiti-pati-gṛha-dvāri manujaiḥ
kriyetānarthajñair viṭa-naṭa-kuṭumbodara-kṛte |
vrajādhīśa-dvāri kṣaṇam api na tiṣṭheyur anaghā
yataḥ sampat-pūrṇā hasati śatamanyor api padam || 47 ||

Word-For-Word Meanings

aviśrāntam – continuously; *sevā* – service; *kṣiti-pati-gṛha-dvāri* – at the door of the residences of kings; *manujaiḥ* – by people; *kriyeta* – is done; *anarthajñaiḥ* – who do not know the meaning of life; *viṭa-naṭa-kuṭumbodara-kṛte* – for the sake of the stomachs of relatives, dancers and paramours; *vrajādhīśa-dvāri* – at the door of the Lord of Vraja; *kṣaṇam* – for a moment; *api* – even; *na* – not; *tiṣṭheyuḥ* – would stand; *anaghā* – faultless; *yataḥ* – whence; *sampat-pūrṇā* – the Goddess of Fortune; *hasati* – laughs at; *śatamanyoḥ* – of Indra; *api* – even; *padam* – position.

Translation

People who do not know the meaning of life continuously serve at the door of the residences of kings in order to fill the stomachs of relatives, dancers and paramours. They do not stand at the door of the Lord of Vraja even for a moment, whence the faultless Goddess of Fortune laughs even at the position of Indra.

TEXT 48

सम्पत्सम्पाद्युतिरिव चला तत्र को वाग्रहः स्याद्
आयुर्वायुप्रतिममिति कस्तत्र विश्वासमेति ।
आरा दाराः क इह हृदि तान् स्थापयेदर्थबुद्ध्या
तस्मादस्मान्नय निजपदं निश्चलं गोकुलेश ॥ ४८ ॥

sampat sampā-dyutir iva calā tatra ko vāgrahaḥ syād
āyur vāyu-pratimam iti kas tatra viśvāsam eti |

ārā dārāḥ ka iha hṛdi tān sthāpayed artha-buddhyā
tasmād asmān naya nija-padaṁ niścalaṁ gokuleśa || 48 ||

Word-For-Word Meanings

sampat – wealth; *sampā-dyutiḥ* – the flash of lightning; *iva* – like; *calā* – flickering; *tatra* – in it; *kaḥ* – what; *vā* – indeed; *āgrahaḥ* – attachment; *syāt* – would be; *āyuḥ* – health; *vāyu-pratimam* – similar to the wind; *iti* – thus; *kaḥ* – who; *tatra* – on it; *viśvāsam* – trust; *eti* – go; *ārāḥ* – knives; *dārāḥ* – wives; *kaḥ* – who; *iha* – in the world; *hṛdi* – in the heart; *tān* – them; *sthāpayet* – would place; *artha-buddhyā* – considering valuable; *tasmāt* – therefore; *asmān* – us; *naya* – bring; *nija-padam* – Your own abode; *niścalam* – steady; *gokuleśa* – O Lord of Gokula.

Translation

Wealth is flickering like the flash of lightning. What is the point in being attached to it? Health is similar to the wind. Who would trust it? Wives are like knives. Who would place them in the heart considering them valuable? Therefore, please bring me to Your own steady abode, O Lord of Gokula.

TEXT 49

अनश्वरषड्रूर्मिमान् विषयनक्रचक्राकुलो
मिलत्तरलभावनाविविधनिम्नगापूरवान् ।
स एव जगदर्णवो गुरुगभीरसम्यज्ञलस्
तितीर्षुरहमस्मि भोस्त्वमसि कर्णधारो हरे ॥ ४९ ॥

anaśvara-ṣaḍ-ūrmimān viṣaya-nakra-cakrākulo
milat-tarala-bhāvanā-vividha-nimna-gāpūravān |
sa eva jagad-arṇavo guru-gabhīra-samyaj-jalas
titīrṣur aham asmi bhos tvam asi karṇa-dhāro hare || 49 ||

Word-For-Word Meanings

anaśvara-ṣaḍ-ūrmimān – having six kinds of imperishable waves; *viṣaya-nakra-cakrākulaḥ* – full of a multitude of crocodiles in the form of sense objects; *milat-tarala-bhāvanā-vividha-nimna-gāpūravān* – in whose depths appear various currents of waves in the form of thoughts; *saḥ* – that; *eva* – indeed; *jagad-arṇavaḥ* – ocean-like material world; *guru-gabhīra-samyaj-jalaḥ* – whose whole waters are extensive and deep; *titīrṣuḥ* – desiring to cross; *aham* – I; *asmi* – am; *bhoḥ* – O; *tvam* – You; *asi* – are; *karṇa-dhāraḥ* – the helmsman; *hare* – O Lord Hari.

Translation

This material world is like an ocean whose whole waters are extensive and deep. It has six imperishable waves,[4] is full of a multitude of crocodiles in the form of sense objects, and in its depths appear various currents of waves in the form of thoughts. I wish to cross such an ocean, and You, O Lord Hari, are the helmsman.

TEXT 50

कुयोनौ नो भीतिर्न जननभयं नो मृतिभयं
विपद्भ्यो वा भीतिर्न च न च जरातो भयमपि ।

4. Lust, anger, greed, illusion, pride and envy.

ममैकासौ भीतिर्नयनपथमेष्यत्यचिरतो
न वा वृन्दारण्यं हरिपदरजःपूतमभितः ॥ ५० ॥

ku-yonau no bhītir na janana-bhayaṁ no mṛti-bhayaṁ
vipadbhyo vā bhītir na ca na ca jarāto bhayam api |
mamaikāsau bhītir nayana-patham eṣyaty acirato
na vā vṛndāraṇyaṁ hari-pada-rajaḥ-pūtam abhitaḥ || 50 ||

Word-For-Word Meanings

ku-yonau – in a low species; *na u* – not; *bhītiḥ* – fear; *na* – nor; *janana-bhayam* – fear of being born again; *na u* – nor; *mṛti-bhayam* – fear of death; *vipadbhyaḥ* – of calamities; *vā* – or; *bhītiḥ* – fear; *na* – nor; *ca* – and; *na* – nor; *ca* – and; *jarātaḥ* – of old age; *bhayam* – fear; *api* – also; *mama* – my; *ekā* – one; *asau* – that; *bhītiḥ* – fear; *nayana-patham* – in the scope of my vision; *eṣyati* – will come; *aciratah* – briefly; *na* – not; *vā* – indeed; *vṛndāraṇyam* – Vṛndāvana; *hari-pada-rajaḥ-pūtam* – which is purified by the dust of the feet of Lord Hari; *abhitaḥ* – completely.

Translation

I have no fear of taking birth again, nor do I fear birth in a low species, nor do I fear death. I have no fear of calamities and not even of old age. I have only one fear – that I may not even briefly see Vṛndāvana, which is completely purified by the dust of the feet of Lord Hari.

TEXT 51

किं विद्याभिस्तपोभिर्धनजनविभवैः कर्मभिर्वा कुलैर्वा
योगैर्धर्मैश्च दानैरपि बहुसुकृतैः क्षेत्रतीर्थावगाहैः ।

न स्याद्गोविन्दपादाम्बुजभजनरुचिर्यद्यनेकार्थदात्री-
पात्रीभूतेन किं वा यदि न हरिजनैः युज्यते सत्सभासु ॥ ५१ ॥

kiṁ vidyābhis tapobhir dhana-jana-vibhavaiḥ karmabhir vā kulair vā
yogair dharmaiś ca dānair api bahu-sukṛtaiḥ kṣetra-tīrthāvagāhaiḥ |
na syād govinda-pādāmbuja-bhajana-rucir yady anekārtha-dātrī-
pātrī-bhūtena kiṁ vā yadi na hari-janaiḥ yujyate sat-sabhāsu || 51 ||

Word-For-Word Meanings

kim – what is the use; *vidyābhiḥ* – of knowledge; *tapobhiḥ* – of austerities; *dhana-jana-vibhavaiḥ* – of wealth, followers and power; *karmabhiḥ* – of work; *vā* – or; *kulaiḥ* – of family; *vā* – or; *yogaiḥ* – of the practice of yoga; *dharmaiḥ* – of religious principles; *ca* – and; *dānaiḥ* – of charity; *api* – and; *bahu-sukṛtaiḥ* – of lots of pious activities; *kṣetra-tīrthāvagāhaiḥ* – of bathing in holy places; *na* – not; *syāt* – would be; *govinda-pādāmbuja-bhajana-ruciḥ* – taste for worshipping the lotus feet of Lord Govinda; *yadi* – if; *anekārtha-dātrī-pātrī-bhūtena* – of giving and receiving many riches; *kim* – what is the use; *vā* – or; *yadi* – if; *na* – not; *hari-janaiḥ* – with Lord Hari's devotees; *yujyate* – is together; *sat-sabhāsu* – in the assemblies of saintly people.

Translation

What is the use of knowledge, austerities, wealth, followers, power, work, family, practice of yoga, religious principles, charity, bathing in holy places and doing lots of pious activities if there is no taste for worshipping the lotus feet of Lord Govinda? What is the use of giving and receiving many riches if one is not together with the devotees of Lord Hari in the assembly of saintly people?

TEXT 52

पुनर्देहो भावी पुनरपि कुटुम्बं पुनरिमे
गृहा दाराः सम्पद्विषयसुखलेशा अपि पुनः ।
स्फुरद्गोपीनेत्रभ्रमरवरपीताननरसे
मुकुन्दे न प्रेमा घननिबिडनीलिम्नि सुलभः ॥ ५२ ॥

punar deho bhāvī punar api kuṭumbaṁ punar ime
gṛhā dārāḥ sampad viṣaya-sukha-leśā api punaḥ |
sphurad-gopī-netra-bhramara-vara-pītānana-rase
mukunde na premā ghana-nibiḍa-nīlimni sulabhaḥ || 52 ||

Word-For-Word Meanings

punaḥ – again; *dehaḥ* – body; *bhāvī* – will be; *punaḥ* – again; *api* – and; *kuṭumbam* – family; *punaḥ* – again; *ime* – these; *gṛhāḥ* – houses; *dārāḥ* – wife; *sampat* – wealth; *viṣaya-sukha-leśā* – whose insignificant happiness is the sense objects; *api* – and; *punaḥ* – again; *sphurad-gopī-netra-bhramara-vara-pītānana-rase* – Whose nectarean face is drunk by the restless eyes of the *gopīs*, which are like the best bumblebees; *mukunde* – for Lord Mukunda; *na* – not; *premā* – love; *ghana-nibiḍa-nīlimni* – deep blue; *sulabhaḥ* – easy to attain.

Translation

If again I will have a body, again a family, again a household, again a wife, and again wealth for insignificant sensual happiness, then it will not be easy to attain love for the deep blue Mukunda, Whose nectarean face is drunk by the restless eyes of the *gopīs*, which are like the best bumblebees.

TEXT 53

सौवर्णाः स्यन्दनौघाः विकटकरिघटाश्चण्डवेगास्तुरङ्गाश्
छत्रं पूर्णेन्दुमित्रं चमरचयचमत्कारचारुप्रचारः ।
राज्यं प्राज्यं दिगन्तावधिनिधिनवकं रूपवत्यो युवत्यो
नैतत्सर्वं व्रजस्त्रीपतिपदभजनानन्दकोट्यंशतुल्यम् ॥ ५३ ॥

sauvarṇāḥ syandanaughāḥ vikaṭa-kari-ghaṭāś caṇḍa-vegās turaṅgāś
chatraṁ pūrṇendu-mitraṁ camara-caya-camatkāra-cāru-pracāraḥ |
rājyaṁ prājyaṁ dig-antāvadhi-nidhi-navakaṁ rūpavatyo yuvatyo
naitat sarvaṁ vraja-strī-pati-pada-bhajanānanda-koṭy-aṁśa-tulyam ||53||

Word-For-Word Meanings

sauvarṇāḥ – golden; *syandanaughāḥ* – fleets of chariots; *vikaṭa-kari-ghaṭāḥ* – herds of huge elephants; *caṇḍa-vegāḥ* – impetuous; *turaṅgāḥ* – horses; *chatram* – an umbrela; *pūrṇendu-mitram* – marked with the sun and the full moon; *camara-caya-camatkāra-cāru-pracāraḥ* – the use of astonishingly beautiful collections of *camaras*; *rājyam* – a kingdom; *prājyam* – great; *dig-antāvadhi-nidhi-navakam* – nine kinds of treasures extending up to the horizon; *rūpavatyaḥ* – beautiful; *yuvatyaḥ* – girls; *na* – not; *etat* – this; *sarvam* – all; *vraja-strī-pati-pada-bhajanānanda-koṭy-aṁśa-tulyam* – compared to a fragment of the bliss of worshipping the lotus feet of the Lord of the ladies of Vraja.

Translation

Fleets of golden chariots, herds of huge elephants, impetuous horses, an umbrella embroidered with the sun and the full moon,[5] the use of astonishingly beautiful collections of *camaras*, a great kingdom, nine kinds of treasures[6] extending up to the horizon, beautiful girls – none of these can compare to a fragment of the bliss of worshipping the lotus feet of the Lord of the ladies of Vraja.

TEXT 54

व्यापारैर्दिवसोऽवसानमगमद्ग्रस्ता निशा निद्रया
धावत्काललुलापलोलचरणाघातो महाभैरवः ।
दुष्प्रापा मथुरापुरी कलिमलप्रक्षालने या क्षमा
गृह्णीते मकरं हरिर्मम ततश्चेतोऽधुना कम्पते ॥ ५४ ॥

vyāpārair divaso 'vasānam agamad grastā niśā nidrayā
dhāvat-kāla-lulāpa-lola-caraṇāghāto mahā-bhairavaḥ |
duṣprāpā mathurā-purī kali-mala-prakṣālane yā kṣamā
gṛhṇīte makaraṁ harir mama tataś ceto 'dhunā kampate || 54 ||

Word-For-Word Meanings

vyāpāraiḥ – with business; *divasaḥ* – the day; *avasānam* – to an end; *agamat* – came; *grastā* – taken; *niśā* – night; *nidrayā* – by sleep; *dhāvat-kāla-lulāpa-lola-caraṇāghātaḥ* –

5. A royal insignia.

6. The nine treasures are those possessed by Kuvera, namely mahāpadma, padma, śaṅkha, makara, kacchapa, mukunda, kunda, nīla and kharva.

striking a running buffalo in the form of time with restless feet; *mahā-bhairavaḥ* – very frightening; *duṣprāpā* – very difficult to attain; *mathurā-purī* – the city of Mathurā; *kali-mala-prakṣālane* – to wash off the impurities of Kali; *yā* – which; *kṣamā* – able; *gṛhṇīte* – snatches; *makaram* – Cupid; *hariḥ* – Lord Hari; *mama* – my; *tataḥ* – because of whom; *cetaḥ* – heart; *adhunā* – now; *kampate* – shakes.

Translation

The day is spent in business and the night is taken by sleep. A very frightening personality[7] with restless feet strikes a running buffalo in the form of time. It is very difficult to attain the city of Mathurā, which is able to wash off the impurities of the Age of Kali and where Lord Hari snatches the Cupid that now makes my heart shake.

TEXT 55

मुकुन्द त्वक्चक्षुःश्रवणरसनघ्राणमददास्
त्वदङ्घ्रिं त्वद्रूपं त्वदनुचरितं त्वद्गुणकथाम् ।
त्वदङ्गस्था मालाः स्पृशति न च पश्यत्यपि तु नो
शृणोति ब्रूते नो न बत परिजिघ्रत्यपि कुधीः ॥ ५५ ॥

mukunda tvak-cakṣuḥ-śravaṇa-rasana-ghrāṇa-mada-dās
tvad-aṅghriṁ tvad-rūpaṁ tvad-anucaritaṁ tvad-guṇa-kathām |
tvad-aṅga-sthā mālāḥ spṛśati na ca paśyaty api tu no
śṛṇoti brūte no na bata parijighraty api kudhīḥ || 55 ||

---

7. Yamarāja, the god of death, whose carrier is a buffalo.

Word-For-Word Meanings

mukunda – O Lord Mukunda; *tvak-cakṣuḥ-śravaṇa-rasana-ghrāṇa-mada-dāḥ* – intoxicating to the nose, tongue, ears, eyes and skin; *tvad-aṅghrim* – Your foot; *tvad-rūpam* – Your form; *tvad-anucaritam* – Your transcendental activities; *tvad-guṇa-kathām* – the narration of Your qualities; *tvad-aṅga-sthāḥ* – placed on Your limbs; *mālāḥ* – garlands; *spṛśati* – touches; *na* – not; *ca* – and; *paśyati* – sees; *api* – and; *tu* – and; *na u* – nor; *śṛṇoti* – hears; *brūte* – speaks; *na u* – nor; *na* – nor; *bata* – alas; *parijighrati* – smells; *api* – and; *kudhīḥ* – a fool.

Translation

O Mukunda, how unfortunate that a foolish person does not touch Your feet, nor sees Your form, nor hears Your transcendental activities, nor narrates Your qualities, nor smells the garlands placed on Your limbs, although they are intoxicating to the nose, tongue, ears, eyes and skin.

TEXT 56

जगद्गाढं ध्वान्तं निरवधि वयं तत्र पतिता
न पश्यामो मार्गं गुणमिह न दोषं न कुधियः ।
भवद्भक्ती रत्नं तदपि तव नाथानुगकरे
त्वदीयानां सङ्गं वितर भगवन्नाशय तमः ॥ ५६ ॥

jagad gāḍhaṁ dhvāntaṁ niravadhi vayaṁ tatra patitā
na paśyāmo mārgaṁ guṇam iha na doṣaṁ na kudhiyaḥ |
bhavad-bhaktī ratnaṁ tad api tava nāthānuga-kare
tvadīyānāṁ saṅgaṁ vitara bhagavan nāśaya tamaḥ || 56 ||

Word-For-Word Meanings

jagat – this material universe; *gāḍham* – deep; *dhvāntam* – dark; *niravadhi* – endless; *vayam* – we; *tatra* – in it; *patitāḥ* – fallen; *na* – not; *paśyāmaḥ* – see; *mārgam* – the path; *guṇam* – virtue; *iha* – here; *na* – nor; *doṣam* – vice; *na* – nor; *kudhiyaḥ* – fools; *bhavad-bhaktī* – devotion for You; *ratnam* – jewel; *tat* – that; *api* – and; *tava* – Your; *nātha* – O Lord; *anuga-kare* – in the hand of Your servant; *tvadīyānām* – of Your devotees; *saṅgam* – association; *vitara* – give; *bhagavan* – O Supreme Lord; *nāśaya* – destroy; *tamaḥ* – darkness.

Translation

This material universe is dense, dark and endless. Fools like us have fallen into it and neither see the path, nor virtues, nor vices. O Lord, the jewel of devotion to You is in the hands of Your servants. O Supreme Lord, please destroy the darkness and give me the association of Your devotees.

TEXT 57

व्रजाधीश त्यक्त्वा तव चरणमन्यं भजति यः
शिलारूढो मूढस्तरति भववार्धिं कथमसौ ।
व्यधुः सर्वे सत्या नयननिमिषस्थायिविषयान्
विलोक्य श्रीवृन्दावननवनिकुञ्जेषु वसतिम् ॥ ५७ ॥

vrajādhīśa tyaktvā tava caraṇam anyaṁ bhajati yaḥ
śilārūḍho mūḍhas tarati bhava-vārdhiṁ katham asau |
vyadhuḥ sarve satyā nayana-nimiṣa-sthāyi-viṣayān
vilokya śrī-vṛndāvana-nava-nikuñjeṣu vasatim || 57 ||

Word-For-Word Meanings

vrajādhīśa – O Lord of Vraja; *tyaktvā* – having given up; *tava* – Your; *caraṇam* – lotus feet; *anyam* – someone else; *bhajati* – worships; *yaḥ* – one who; *śilārūḍhaḥ* – riding on a rock; *mūḍhaḥ* – fool; *tarati* – crosses; *bhava-vārdhim* – the ocean of material existence; *katham* – how; *asau* – that; *vyadhuḥ* – did; *sarve* – all; *satyāḥ* – saintly persons; *nayana-nimiṣa-sthāyi-viṣayān* – sensual pleasures, which last for a twinkling of an eye; *vilokya* – having observed; *śrī-vṛndāvana-nava-nikuñjeṣu* – in the fresh bowers of Śrī Vṛndāvana; *vasatim* – residence.

Translation

O Lord of Vraja, giving up Your lotus feet and worshipping someone else, how can such a fool cross the ocean of material existence riding on a rock? Having observed that sensual pleasures last for the mere twinkling of an eye, all saintly persons have made their residence in the fresh bowers of Śrī Vṛndāvana.

TEXT 58

ईर्ष्यामत्सरमोहमानचरणो लोभाधरौष्ठान्वितः
कामक्रोधरदो मदोग्ररसनो मायोग्रशुण्डाधरः ।
विभ्राणः सुखदुःखकुम्भयुगलं सम्पद्विपत्कर्णयुग्
भीमोऽयं कलिकालकुञ्जरवरः कृष्णोऽस्ति पञ्चाननः ॥ ५८ ॥

īrṣyā-matsara-moha-māna-caraṇo lobhādharauṣṭhānvitaḥ
kāma-krodha-rado madogra-rasano māyogra-śuṇḍādharaḥ |

vibhrāṇaḥ sukha-duḥkha-kumbha-yugalaṁ sampad-vipat-karṇa-yug
bhīmo 'yaṁ kali-kāla-kuñjara-varaḥ kṛṣṇo 'sti pañcānanaḥ || 58 ||

Word-For-Word Meanings

īrṣyā-matsara-moha-māna-caraṇaḥ – whose feet are envy, jealousy, bewilderment and pride; *lobhādharauṣṭhānvitaḥ* – whose lips are greed; *kāma-krodha-radaḥ* – whose tusks are lust and anger; *madogra-rasanaḥ* – whose terrific tongue is madness; *māyogra-śuṇḍādharaḥ* – whose formidable trunk is illusion; *vibhrāṇaḥ* – opening wide its mouth; *sukha-duḥkha-kumbha-yugalam* – whose two sides of the forehead are happiness and distress; *sampad-vipat-karṇa-yuk* – whose ears are good fortune and calamity; *bhīmaḥ* – terrible; *ayam* – this; *kali-kāla-kuñjara-varaḥ* – the best of elephants in the form of the Age of Kali; *kṛṣṇaḥ* – Lord Kṛṣṇa; *asti* – is; *pañcānanaḥ* – lion.

Translation

This terrible Age of Kali is like the best of elephants opening wide its mouth. Envy, jealousy, bewilderment and pride are its feet; greed is its lips; lust and anger are its tusks; madness is its terrific tongue; illusion is its formidable trunk; happiness and distress are the two sides of its forehead; and good fortune and calamity are its ears. Lord Kṛṣṇa, however, is like a lion.

TEXT 59

कामक्रोधचपेटपीडनकरो दैन्यार्तिदंष्ट्राशतो
लोभस्फारकरालदृग्ज्वरजराजिह्वोऽनृतप्रेक्षणः ।

आधिव्याधिनखो विषादनिनदः संसारसिंहो बली
शक्तस्तद्दमनाय नन्दतनयः पाता किमन्यो भुवि ॥ ५९ ॥

kāma-krodha-capeṭa-pīḍana-karo dainyārti-daṁṣṭrā-śato
lobha-sphāra-karāla-dṛg jvara-jarā-jihvo 'nṛta-prekṣaṇaḥ |
ādhi-vyādhi-nakho viṣāda-ninadaḥ saṁsāra-siṁho balī
śaktas tad-damanāya nanda-tanayaḥ pātā kim anyo bhuvi || 59 ||

Word-For-Word Meanings

kāma-krodha-capeṭa-pīḍana-karaḥ – whose paws are the affliction caused by blows of lust and anger; *dainyārti-daṁṣṭrā-śataḥ* –whose hundreds of teeth are dejection and grief; *lobha-sphāra-karāla-dṛk* – whose large terrible eyes are greed; *jvara-jarā-jihvaḥ* – whose tongue is fever and old age; *anṛta-prekṣaṇaḥ* – whose sight is falsehood; *ādhi-vyādhi-nakhaḥ* – whose nails are anxiety and disease; *viṣāda-ninadaḥ* – whose roar is despair; *saṁsāra-siṁhaḥ* – the lion-like cycle of material existence; *balī* – powerfull; *śaktaḥ* – able; *tad-damanāya* – to tame it; *nanda-tanayaḥ* – the son of Nanda Mahārāja; *pātā* – protector; *kim* – what; *anyaḥ* – other; *bhuvi* – in this world.

Translation

The cycle of material existence is like a powerful lion. Its paws are the affliction caused by blows of lust and anger; its hundreds of teeth are dejection and grief; its large terrible eyes are greed; its tongue is fever and old age; its sight is falsehood; anxiety and disease are its nails; despair is its roar. Is there any protector in this world able to tame it except for the son of Nanda Mahārāja?

TEXT 60

तपो योगं यागं व्रतसुकृततीर्थानि कुरुतां
तुलादिब्रह्माण्डावधिसविधिदानानि ददताम् ।
लसद्गोपीवृन्दप्रियतमविहाराङ्गनपदं
विना वृन्दारण्यं न गतिमपरत्रैति पुरुषः ॥ ६० ॥

tapo yogaṁ yāgaṁ vrata-sukṛta-tīrthāni kurutāṁ
tulādi-brahmāṇḍāvadhi-savidhi-dānāni dadatām |
lasad-gopī-vṛnda-priyatama-vihārāṅgana-padaṁ
vinā vṛndāraṇyaṁ na gatim aparatraiti puruṣaḥ || 60 ||

Word-For-Word Meanings

tapaḥ – austerity; *yogam* – yoga; *yāgam* – sacrifice; *vrata-sukṛta-tīrthāni* – religious vows, pious activities and pilgrimage to holy places; *kurutām* – may do; *tulādi-brahmāṇḍāvadhi-savidhi-dānāni* – charity according to the scriptural injunctions starting with things measured on a scale up to a whole universe; *dadatām* – may give; *lasad-gopī-vṛnda-priyatama-vihārāṅgana-padam* – the abode where the beloved of the sportive groups of *gopīs* walks and performs pastimes; *vinā* – without; *vṛndāraṇyam* – Vṛndāvana; *na* – not; *gatim* – the goal of life; *aparatra* – anywhere else; *eti* – attains; *puruṣaḥ* – a person.

Translation

Let one perform austerities, yoga, sacrifices, religious vows, pious activities and pilgrimage to holy places. Let one give charity according to the scriptural injunctions starting with things measured on a scale up to a whole universe. Without Vṛndāvana, the abode where the beloved of the sportive *gopīs* walks and performs pastimes, one cannot attain the ultimate goal of life anywhere else.

TEXT 61

कीदृग्भक्तिस्त्वयि समुचिता सन्ति के तत्प्रभेदाः
को वा सम्यग्जनयति फलं सम्प्रदायाख्यवृक्षः ।
नाहं जाने किमपि भगवञ् जीवमात्रप्रभुस्त्वं
सर्वे दासास्तव जगदिदं त्वत्कृतं नाथ जाने ॥ ६१ ॥

kīdṛg bhaktis tvayi samucitā santi ke tat-prabhedāḥ
ko vā samyag janayati phalaṁ sampradāyākhya-vṛkṣaḥ |
nāhaṁ jāne kim api bhagavañ jīva-mātra-prabhus tvaṁ
sarve dāsās tava jagad idaṁ tvat-kṛtaṁ nātha jāne || 61 ||

Word-For-Word Meanings

kīdṛk – which kind; *bhaktiḥ* – devotion; *tvayi* – for You; *samucitā* – proper; *santi* – are; *ke* – what; *tat-prabhedāḥ* – its divisions; *kaḥ* – what; *vā* – and; *samyak* – real; *janayati* – produces; *phalam* – fruit; *sampradāyākhya-vṛkṣaḥ* – the tree called disciplic succession; *na* – not; *aham* – I; *jāne* – know; *kim api* – anything; *bhagavan* – O Supreme Lord; *jīva-mātra-prabhuḥ* – the master of all living entities; *tvam* – You; *sarve* – all; *dāsāḥ* – servants; *tava* – Your; *jagat* – universe; *idam* – this; *tvat- kṛtam* – made by You; *nātha* – O Lord; *jāne* – I know.

Translation

Which kind of devotion for You is proper? What are its divisions? What is the real fruit produced by the tree called disciplic succession? O Supreme Lord, I know that this universe is made by You and that You are the master of all living entities and everyone is Your servant. I do not know anything else, O Lord.

TEXT 62

कृतघ्ना ये जीवा स्वशिरसि निदेशं न दधते
वदन्तो वेदार्थं त्रिदिवफलहेतुक्रतुपरम् ।
निरालम्बाः स्वर्गात्पतनमनुभूय त्रिभुवने
लभन्ते दुःखादप्यधिकतरदुःखं कुमतयः ॥ ६२ ॥

kṛta-ghnā ye jīvā sva-śirasi nideśaṁ na dadhate
vadanto vedārthaṁ tri-diva-phala-hetu-kratu-param |
nirālambāḥ svargāt patanam anubhūya tri-bhuvane
labhante duḥkhād apy adhikatara-duḥkhaṁ kumatayaḥ || 62 ||

Word-For-Word Meanings

kṛta-ghnāḥ – ungrateful; *ye* – those; *jīvāḥ* – living entities; *sva-śirasi* – on their heads; *nideśam* – instruction; *na* – not; *dadhate* – take; *vadantaḥ* – speaking; *vedārtham* – the import of the Vedas; *tri-diva-phala-hetu-kratu-param* – in terms of sacrifices that result in attainment of the heavenly planets; *nirālambāḥ* – having no support; *svargāt* – from heaven; *patanam* – fall; *anubhūya* – after experiencing; *tri-bhuvane* – in the three worlds; *labhante* – obtain; *duḥkhāt* – than suffering; *api* – even; *adhikatara-duḥkham* – more suffering; *kumatayaḥ* – fools.

Translation

Ungrateful living entities do not take Your instruction on their heads and simply speak of the import of the Vedas in terms of sacrifices that result in attainment of the heavenly planets. Such fools have no support anywhere in the three worlds, and after falling down from heaven, they obtain even more suffering.

TEXT 63

अजानन्तो लोका अहमपि न जानामि कुमतिस्
त्वदीयं पन्थानं विविधमतिभेदेन विदुषाम् ।
अतस्त्वं किं तत्त्वं किमिति तव पादैकशरणं
प्रयातोऽहं मोहं शमय मम कुञ्जप्रियविभो ॥ ६३ ॥

ajānanto lokā aham api na jānāmi kumatis
tvadīyaṁ panthānaṁ vividha-mati-bhedena viduṣām |
atas tvaṁ kiṁ tattvaṁ kim iti tava pādaika-śaraṇaṁ
prayāto 'haṁ mohaṁ śamaya mama kuñja-priya-vibho || 63 ||

Word-For-Word Meanings

ajānantaḥ – no knowing; *lokāḥ* – people; *aham* – I; *api* – also; *na* – not; *jānāmi* – know; *kumatiḥ* – fool; *tvadīyam* – Your; *panthānam* – path; *vividha-mati-bhedena* – according to many different views; *viduṣām* – of learned scholars; *ataḥ* – therefore; *tvam* – You; *kim* – what; *tattvam* – the truth; *kim* – what; *iti* – thus; *tava* – Your; *pādaika-śaraṇam* – exclusive shelter at Your feet; *prayātaḥ* – come; *aham* – I;

moham – illusion; *śamaya* – remove; *mama* – my; *kuñja-priya-vibho* – O Lord fond of bowers.

Translation

Just as common people do not know Your path as presented by learned scholars according to many different views, this fool too does not. Therefore, as I have taken exclusive shelter at Your feet, O Lord fond of bowers, please remove this illusion of mine: Who are You? What is the truth?

TEXT 64

अनित्यं वा नित्यं भवतु जगदेतन्न विवदे
विनाशार्हो नात्मा तव चरणसेवा प्रतिजनुः ।
प्रपञ्चातीतस्त्वं चरितमपि तादृक्तव विभो
विवादो न त्वय्यात्मनि मयि न देहे भवतु सः ॥ ६४ ॥

anityaṁ vā nityaṁ bhavatu jagad etan na vivade
vināśārho nātmā tava caraṇa-sevā pratijanuḥ |
prapañcātītas tvaṁ caritam api tādṛk tava vibho
vivādo na tvayy ātmani mayi na dehe bhavatu saḥ || 64 ||

Word-For-Word Meanings

anityam – non-eternal; *vā* – or; *nityam* – eternal; *bhavatu* – let there be; *jagat* – material universe; *etat* – this; *na* – not; *vivade* – contend; *vināśārhaḥ* – subject to destruction; *na* – not; *ātmā* – soul; *tava* – Your; *caraṇa-sevā* – service to the feet; *pratijanuḥ* – birth after birth; *prapañcātītaḥ* – beyond the material creation; *tvam* – You; *caritam* – activities; *api* –

also; *tādṛk* – similar; *tava* – Your; *vibho* – O Lord; *vivādaḥ* – controversy; *na* – not; *tvayi* – about You; *ātmani* – about the soul; *mayi* – about me; *na* – not; *dehe* – about the body; *bhavatu* – let there be; *saḥ* – that.

Translation

I do not contend whether this material universe is eternal or otherwise. The soul is certainly never subject to destruction, therefore let there be service to Your lotus feet birth after birth. You are beyond the material creation and so are Your activities, O Lord. Let there be no controversy regarding You, me – the spirit soul – and this material body.

TEXT 65

अनित्यज्ञानेच्छाप्रयतनशरीरादिरभवं
तवैतत्कालेषु त्रिषु भगवतो नित्यमखिलम् ।
त्वमीशोऽनीशोऽहं व्रजकुलज माया तव वशे
वशेऽहं मायाया इति तदपिधानाय भजनम् ॥ ६५ ॥

anitya-jñānecchā-prayatana-śarīrādir abhavaṁ
tavaitat kāleṣu triṣu bhagavato nityam akhilam |
tvam īśo 'nīśo 'haṁ vraja-kulaja māyā tava vaśe
vaśe 'haṁ māyāyā iti tad-apidhānāya bhajanam || 65 ||

Word-For-Word Meanings

anitya-jñānecchā-prayatana-śarīrādiḥ – a combination of temporary elements such as body, knowledge, desire, effort, etc.; *abhavam* – became; *tava* – Your; *etat* – this;

kāleṣu – times; *triṣu* – three; *bhagavataḥ* – of the Supreme Lord; *nityam* – eternal; *akhilam* – all; *tvam* – You; *īśaḥ* – Master; *anīśaḥ* – not a master; *aham* – I; *vraja-kulaja* – O Lord born in Vraja; *māyā* – the illusory energy; *tava* – Your; *vaśe* – under control; *aham* – I; *māyāyāḥ* – of the illusory energy; *iti* – thus; *tad-apidhānāya* – to remove it; *bhajanam* – worship.

Translation

I became a combination of temporary elements such as body, knowledge, desire, effort, etc., while You, being the Supreme Lord, have a body, knowledge, etc. which exist eternally in the past, present and future. O Lord born in Vraja, You are the Master, I am not. The illusory energy is under Your control, but I am under the control of Your illusory energy, and Your worship is the means to remove it.

TEXT 66

दत्ते भक्तिरसं करोति विरसं चेतः प्रपञ्चाध्वनि
स्वानन्दं तनुते तमो विधुनुते दूरं क्षिपत्यापदः ।
सत्सङ्गाभिरतिं ददाति मथुरा मथ्नाति मानार्णवं
मामेतां नय गोपिनाथ चरणाम्भोजे दिदृक्षा तव ॥ ६६ ॥

datte bhakti-rasaṁ karoti virasaṁ cetaḥ prapañcādhvani
svānandaṁ tanute tamo vidhunute dūraṁ kṣipaty āpadaḥ |
sat-saṅgābhiratiṁ dadāti mathurā mathnāti mānārṇavaṁ
mām etāṁ naya gopinātha caraṇāmbhoje didṛkṣā tava || 66 ||

Word-For-Word Meanings

datte – gives; *bhakti-rasam* – a taste for devotional service; *karoti* – makes; *virasam* – tasteless; *cetaḥ* – the mind; *prapañcādhvani* – in the path of material existence; *svānandam* – Your blissfulness; *tanute* – spreads; *tamaḥ* – darkness; *vidhunute* – removes; *dūram* – far away; *kṣipati* – throws; *āpadaḥ* – calamities; *sat-saṅgābhiratim* – the pleasure of saintly association; *dadāti* – gives; *mathurā* – Mathurā; *mathnāti* – churns; *mānārṇavam* – the ocean of honour; *mām* – me; *etām* – to it; *naya* – bring; *gopinātha* – O Gopīnātha; *caraṇāmbhoje* – lotus feet; *didṛkṣā* – desire to see; *tava* – Your.

Translation

Mathurā gives a taste for Your devotional service and makes one's mind feel no taste for the path of material existence. It spreads Your blissfulness, removes darkness and throws all calamities far away. It gives the pleasure of saintly association and churns the ocean of honour. O Gopīnātha, please bring me to Mathurā, for I have a desire to see Your lotus feet.

TEXT 67

चलदलजलमित्रे न स्थिरत्वं शरीरे
मनसि तव दिदृक्षा स्थास्यति प्राणनाथ ।
इति मम परितोषो नो जने भोजने वा
न भवति निशि घस्रे नो गृहे नो बहिर्वा ॥ ६७ ॥

cala-dala-jala-mitre na sthiratvaṁ śarīre
manasi tava didṛkṣā sthāsyati prāṇanātha |
iti mama paritoṣo no jane bhojane vā
na bhavati niśi ghasre no gṛhe no bahir vā || 67 ||

Word-For-Word Meanings

cala-dala-jala-mitre – in the sun reflected on the water contained on a shaking leaf; *na* – not; *sthiratvam* – permanence; *śarīre* – in this body; *manasi* – in the heart; *tava* – Your; *didṛkṣā* – desire to see; *sthāsyati* – will remain; *prāṇanātha* – O Lord of my life; *iti* – thus; *mama* – my; *paritoṣaḥ* – satisfaction; *na u* – not; *jane* – among relatives; *bhojane* – in food; *vā* – or; *na* – not; *bhavati* – there is; *niśi* – at night; *ghasre* – during the day; *na u* – nor; *gṛhe* – at home; *na u* – nor; *bahiḥ* – outside; *vā* – either.

Translation

There is no permanence in this body, which is like a reflection of the sun on the water contained on a shaking leaf. O Lord of my life, the desire to see You will remain in my heart. Therefore, I do not find satisfaction among relatives, in foodstuffs, in the day, at night, at home or outside.

TEXT 68

कुजनपरिवृतोऽहं प्रत्यहं नाथ कम्पे
वृकवृत इव भीतो निर्जने चाग एकः ।
त्वमसि शरण एकस्तस्य मे दीनबन्धो
सदनवननिषण्णः पूत्करोम्यग्रतस्ते ॥ ६८ ॥

kujana-parivṛto 'haṁ pratyahaṁ nātha kampe
vṛka-vṛta iva bhīto nirjane chāga ekaḥ |
tvam asi śaraṇa ekas tasya me dīna-bandho
sadana-vana-niṣaṇṇaḥ pūt karomy agratas te || 68 ||

Word-For-Word Meanings

kujana-parivṛtaḥ – surrounded by wicked people; *aham* – I; *pratyaham* – daily; *nātha* – O Lord; *kampe* – I tremble; *vṛka-vṛtaḥ* – surrounded by wolves; *iva* – like; *bhītaḥ* – affraid; *nirjane* – in a desolate place; *chāgaḥ* – goat; *ekaḥ* – one; *tvam* – You; *asi* – are; *śaraṇaḥ* – shelter; *ekaḥ* – only; *tasya* – of this; *me* – my; *dīna-bandho* – O friend of the distressed; *sadana-vana-niṣaṇṇaḥ* – sitting in a forest-like home; *pūt karomi* – breath heavily; *agrataḥ* – in front; *te* – You.

Translation

O Lord, daily surrounded by wicked people, I tremble in fear just like a goat surrounded by wolves in a desolate place. O friend of the distressed, You are my only shelter. Sitting in a forest-like home, I am breathing heavily before You.

TEXT 69

गृहसरसि गभीरे कामनानक्रचक्र-
प्रमथितचरणोऽहं शोकदैन्यार्तितप्तः ।
गजमिव कृपया मामुद्धर प्राणबन्धो
करिण इव न किञ्चिद्बन्धवः कर्तुमीशाः ॥ ६९ ॥

gṛha-sarasi gabhīre kāmanā-nakra-cakra-
pramathita-caraṇo 'haṁ śoka-dainyārti-taptaḥ |
gajam iva kṛpayā mām uddhara prāṇa-bandho
kariṇa iva na kiñcid bandhavaḥ kartum īśāḥ || 69 ||

Word-For-Word Meanings

gṛha-sarasi – lake-like home; *gabhīre* – deep; *kāmanā-nakra-cakra-pramathita-caraṇaḥ* – whose feet are being injured by a multitude of crocodile-like desires; *aham* – I; *śoka-dainyārti-taptaḥ* – afflicted by pain, dejection and grief; *gajam* – elephant; *iva* – like; *kṛpayā* – kindly; *mām* – me; *uddhara* – rescue; *prāṇa-bandho* – O friend of my life; *kariṇaḥ* – elephants; *iva* – like; *na* – not; *kiñcit* – anything; *bandhavaḥ* – relatives; *kartum* – to do; *īśāḥ* – able.

Translation

In this deep lake called home, I am afflicted by pain, dejection and grief, and my feet are being injured by a multitude of crocodile-like desires. O beloved friend, kindly rescue me, who am just like an elephant. My elephant-like relatives are not able to do anything.

TEXT 70

लभे लब्धं लप्स्ये नृपतिरतिमानं वितनुते
करिष्ये कुर्वेऽहं कृतमिति मया कृत्यमखिलम् ।
इति व्यामोहेन क्षयितमिदमायुर्जडधिया
स्मृतो न त्वं नाथ क्षणमपि ततो दुःखमगमम् ॥ ७० ॥

labhe labdhaṁ lapsye nṛ-patir ati-mānaṁ vitanute
kariṣye kurve 'haṁ kṛtam iti mayā kṛtyam akhilam |
iti vyāmohena kṣayitam idam āyur jaḍa-dhiyā
smṛto na tvaṁ nātha kṣaṇam api tato duḥkham agamam || 70 ||

Word-For-Word Meanings

labhe – I am getting; *labdham* – gotten; *lapsye* – I will get; *nṛ-pati-rati-mānam* – the king's affection and respect; *vitanute* – causes; *kariṣye* – I will do; *kurve* – I am doing; *aham* – I; *kṛtam* – done; *iti* – thus; *mayā* – by me; *kṛtyam* – to be done; *akhilam* – all; *iti* – thus; *vyāmohena* – by bewilderment; *kṣayitam* – ruined; *idam* – this; *āyuḥ* – life span; *jaḍa- dhiyā* – by this fool; *smṛtaḥ* – remembered; *na* – not; *tvam* – You; *nātha* – O Lord; *kṣaṇam* – a moment; *api* – even; *tataḥ* – therefore; *duḥkham* – suffering; *agamam* – I attained.

Translation

"I got that, I am getting this, I will get that too. I've done that, I am doing this, I will do that, which will earn me the king's affection and respect. I have all this to do." Fool as I am, my life span has been ruined by such bewilderment. O Lord, I did not remember You even for a moment and therefore attained only suffering.

TEXT 71

तर्के केचन कर्कशोक्तिचतुरा जल्पेऽप्यनल्पाननाः
केचिद्वाक्छलजातिनिग्रहवितण्डासु प्रचण्डाः परे ।

केचिद् धूमहुताशपर्वतकथामायुःक्षयं जानते
श्रीकृष्णाद्भुतवर्णनासु विमुखाः शोचामि तान् पण्डितान् ॥ ७१ ॥

tarke kecana karkaśokti-caturā jalpe 'py analpānanāḥ
kecid vāk-chala-jāti-nigraha-vitaṇḍāsu pracaṇḍāḥ pare |
kecid dhūma-hutāśa-parvata-kathām āyuḥ-kṣayaṁ jānate
śrī-kṛṣṇādbhuta-varṇanāsu vimukhāḥ śocāmi tān paṇḍitān || 71 ||

Word-For-Word Meanings

tarke – in logic; *kecana* – some people; *karkaśokti-caturāḥ* – very skilful in using strong words; *jalpe* – in wrangling; *api* – and; *analpānanāḥ* – talkative; *kecit* – some; *vāk-chala-jāti-nigraha-vitaṇḍāsu* – in quibbling, giving futile answers, pointing out flaws in the arguments, and presenting captious arguments; *pracaṇḍāḥ* – very strong; *pare* – others; *kecit* – some; *dhūma-hutāśa-parvata-kathām* – the anecdote that there must be fire on the hill since there is smoke; *āyuḥ-kṣayam* – the end of their life span; *jānate* – know; *śrī-kṛṣṇādbhuta-varṇanāsu* – towards the wonderful descriptions about Lord Śrī Kṛṣṇa; *vimukhāḥ* – averse; *śocāmi* – I take pity; *tān* – them; *paṇḍitān* – scholars.

Translation

Some people are very skilful in using strong words and logic; some talkative people are skilful in wrangling (jalpa); others are very strong in quibbling (vāk-chala), giving futile answers (jāti), pointing out flaws in the arguments (nigraha), and presenting captious arguments (vitaṇḍā); and there are others who know the anecdote that there must be fire on the hill since there is smoke.

They experience the end of their life span in this way. I take pity on all these scholars who are averse to the wonderful descriptions about Lord Śrī Kṛṣṇa.

TEXT 72

नाहं न्यायमते विशामि न पुनर्मीमांसकानां मते
नो वेदान्तमते न सांख्यविदुषां तत्तन्मते मन्दधीः ।
श्यामाङ्गं मृदुवेणुवादनरतं गोपीकदम्बान्वितं
कृष्णं नौमि नमामि यामि शरणं ध्यायामि गायामि च ॥ ७२ ॥

nāhaṁ nyāya-mate viśāmi na punar mīmāṁsakānāṁ mate
no vedānta-mate na sāṁkhya-viduṣāṁ tat-tan-mate manda-dhīḥ |
śyāmāṅgaṁ mṛdu-veṇu-vādana-rataṁ gopī-kadambānvitaṁ
kṛṣṇaṁ naumi namāmi yāmi śaraṇaṁ dhyāyāmi gāyāmi ca || 72 ||

Word-For-Word Meanings

na – not; *aham* – I; *nyāya-mate* – in the Nyāya philosophy; *viśāmi* – enter into; *na* – not; *punaḥ* – moreover; *mīmāṁsakānām* – of the followers of Mīmāṁsā; *mate* – in the philosophy; *na u* – nor; *vedānta-mate* – in the philosophy of Vedānta; *na* – nor; *sāṁkhya-viduṣām* – of the scholars of Sāṁkhya; *tat-tan-mate* – in their respective philosophies; *manda-dhīḥ* – dull-headed; *śyāmāṅgam* – Whose bodily hue is deep blue; *mṛdu-veṇu-vādana-ratam* – Who is fond of playing a delicate flute; *gopī-kadambānvitam* – accompanied by a group of cowherd girls; *kṛṣṇam* – to Lord Kṛṣṇa; *naumi* – I glorify; *namāmi* – I bow down; *yāmi* – I go; *śaraṇam* – shelter; *dhyāyāmi* – I meditate; *gāyāmi* – I sing; *ca* – and.

Translation

I am dull-headed and do not know much of Nyāya philosophy, nor the philosophy of the followers of Mīmāṁsā, nor the philosophy of Vedānta, nor the philosophy of the scholars of Sāṁkhya. I simply glorify, bow down, take shelter of, meditate on, and sing about Lord Kṛṣṇa, Whose bodily hue is deep blue, Who is fond of playing a delicate flute and is accompanied by a group of cowherd girls.

TEXT 73

तत्तच्छस्त्रमतप्रविष्टमतयो जानन्तु सर्वं बुधा
जल्पाजल्पकथा वदन्त्वपि मिथः स्पर्धिष्णवो वादिनः ।
जानीमो वयमेकमेव न परं वृन्दावनस्थायिनं
राधारासविलासलोलमनसं श्रीनन्दगोपात्मजम् ॥ ७३ ॥

tat-tac-chāstra-mata-praviṣṭa-matayo jānantu sarvaṁ budhā
jalpājalpa-kathā vadantv api mithaḥ spardhiṣṇavo vādinaḥ |
jānīmo vayam ekam eva na paraṁ vṛndāvana-sthāyinaṁ
rādhā-rāsa-vilāsa-lola-manasaṁ śrī-nanda-gopātmajam || 73 ||

Word-For-Word Meanings

tat-tac-chāstra-mata-praviṣṭa-matayaḥ – whose minds have taken to the philosophy of their respective treatises; *jānantu* – may know; *sarvam* – all this; *budhāḥ* – the learned scholars; *jalpājalpa-kathāḥ* – argue back and forth; *vadantu* – may talk; *api* – and; *mithaḥ* – with one another; *spardhiṣṇavaḥ* – disputant; *vādinaḥ* – philosophers; *jānīmaḥ* – know; *vayam* – we; *ekam* – one; *eva* – only; *na* –

not; *param* – something else; *vṛndāvana-sthāyinam* – Who lives in Vṛndāvana; *rādhā-rāsa-vilāsa-lola-manasam* – Whose mind is always eager to enjoy the *rāsa* pastimes with Śrīmatī Rādhārāṇī; *śrī-nanda-gopātmajam* – the son of Nanda Mahārāja.

Translation

Let the learned scholars who have taken to the philosophy of their respective treatises know all this. Let the disputant philosophers argue back and forth in various ways with one another. All I know is the son of Nanda Mahārāja, Who lives in Vṛndāvana and Whose mind is always eager to enjoy the *rāsa* pastimes with Śrīmatī Rādhārāṇī, nothing else.

TEXT 74

नालङ्कारे न काव्ये कुशलमतिरहं नाटके नो पटुर्वा
नो वा शास्त्रे विदग्धो न निगमचतुरः शब्दविद्यां न जाने ।
श्रृङ्गाराङ्गेषु मूढः प्रविशति न मतिः कोशनाट्यादिशास्त्रे
श्रीराधानाथनाम प्रतिघटि मनुजैर्वाच्यमेतद्धि वेद्मि ॥ ७४ ॥

nālaṅkāre na kāvye kuśala-matir ahaṁ nāṭake no paṭur vā
no vā śāstre vidagdho na nigama-caturaḥ śabda-vidyāṁ na jāne |
śṛṅgārāṅgeṣu mūḍhaḥ praviśati na matiḥ kośa-nāṭyādi-śāstre
śrī-rādhā-nātha-nāma pratighaṭi manujair vācyam etaddhi vedmi ||74||

Word-For-Word Meanings

na – not; *alaṅkāre* – in figures of speech; *na* – nor; *kāvye* – in poetry; *kuśala-matiḥ* – well versed; *aham* – I; *nāṭake* – in drama; *na u* – nor; *paṭuḥ* – proficient; *vā* – or; *na u* – not; *vā* – or; *śāstre* – in scriptures; *vidagdhaḥ* – scholar; *na* – nor; *nigama-caturaḥ* – skilful in the Vedas; *śabda-vidyām* – philology; *na* – not; *jāne* – know; *śṛṅgārāṅgeṣu* – in the different divisions of erotic sentiments in literature; *mūḍhaḥ* – ignorant; *praviśati* – has access; *na* – not; *matiḥ* – mind; *kośa-nāṭyādi-śāstre* – in texts on lexicography, dance, etc.; *śrī-rādhā-nātha-nāma* – the Holy Name of the Lord of Śrīmatī Rādhārāṇī; *pratighaṭi* – at every moment; *manujaiḥ* – by everyone; *vācyam* – to be uttered; *etat* – this; *hi* – only; *vedmi* – I know.

Translation

I am neither well-versed in the figures of speech or poetry, nor am I proficient in drama. I am neither a scholar of the scriptures, nor skilful in the Vedas, and I also do not know philology. I am ignorant of the different divisions of erotic sentiments in literature, and my mind does not have access to texts on lexicography, dance, etc. All I know is that the Holy Name of the Lord of Śrīmatī Rādhārāṇī should be uttered by everyone at every moment.

TEXT 75

शास्त्रं निन्दामि नाहं न च विबुधजनांस्तन्मताभ्यासकर्तॄन्
भिन्ना तत्तज्ञनानां रुचिरिह जनता नैकमत्ये स्थितासौ ।
श्रीमद्वृन्दावनश्रीनवललितलतामण्डपाडम्बरस्थ-
श्रीराधाकान्तपादाम्बुजभजनरुचिर्जन्मकोटौ ममास्तु ॥ ७५ ॥

śāstraṁ nindāmi nāhaṁ na ca vibudha-janāṁs tan-matābhyāsa-kartṝn
bhinnā tat-taj-janānāṁ rucir iha janatā naikamatye sthitāsau |
śrīmad-vṛndāvana-śrī-nava-lalita-latā-maṇḍapāḍambara-stha-
śrī-rādhā-kānta-pādāmbuja-bhajana-rucir janma-koṭau mamāstu || 75 ||

Word-For-Word Meanings

śāstram – scripture; *nindāmi* – condemn; *na* – not; *aham* – I; *na* – nor; *ca* – and; *vibudha-janān* – the learned scholars; *tan-matābhyāsa-kartṝn* – who study these philosophies; *bhinnā* – different; *tat-taj-janānām* – of all these different people; *ruciḥ* – taste; *iha* – in this world; *janatā* – people; *na* – not; *ekamatye* – on a single view; *sthitā* – fixed; *asau* – that; *śrīmad-vṛndāvana- śrī- nava- lalita- latā- maṇḍapāḍambara- stha- śrī- rādhā-kānta- pādāmbuja- bhajana- ruciḥ* – taste for the worship of the lotus feet of the beloved of Śrīmatī Rādhārāṇī, Who is always feeling pleasure in the bowers of fresh, beautiful creepers in Śrī Vṛndāvana; *janma-koṭau* – in millions of births; *mama* – my; *astu* – let there be.

Translation

I neither condemn all these treatises, nor the learned scholars who study these philosophies. All of them have different tastes, for actually in this world people are not fixed on a single view. For millions of lives, may I have a taste for the worship of the lotus feet of the beloved of Śrīmatī Rādhārāṇī, Who is always feeling pleasure in the bowers of fresh, beautiful creepers in Śrī Vṛndāvana.

TEXT 76

नानाशास्त्रविचारचारुमतयो विद्वज्जनाः क्व क्व वा
क्वाहं मन्दमतिर्नवीनजलदश्यामस्पृहारूढधीः ।
नाकाङ्क्षामि कुलं धनं न विभुतां मानं न नो सम्पदं
वृन्दारण्यकलिन्दजाजलतटे जन्मास्तु लक्षावधि ॥ ७६ ॥

nānā-śāstra-vicāra-cāru-matayo vidvaj-janāḥ kva kva vā
kvāhaṁ manda-matir navīna-jalada-śyāma-spṛhārūḍha-dhīḥ |
nākāṅkṣāmi kulaṁ dhanaṁ na vibhutāṁ mānaṁ na no sampadaṁ
vṛndāraṇya-kalinda-jā-jala-taṭe janmāstu lakṣāvadhi || 76 ||

Word-For-Word Meanings

nānā-śāstra-vicāra-cāru-matayaḥ – whose sophisticated minds are engaged in reflecting on various treatises; *vidvaj-janāḥ* – learned scholars; *kva*- where; *kva* – where; *vā* – and; *kva* – where; *aham* – I; *manda-matiḥ* – fool; *navīna-jalada-śyāma-spṛhārūḍha-dhīḥ* – whose mind is fixed on the desire for Śyāma, Whose hue is like that of a new cloud; *na* – not; *ākāṅkṣāmi* – long for; *kulam* – family; *dhanam* – wealth; *na* – nor; *vibhutām* – power; *mānam* – respect; *na* – nor; *na u* – nor; *sampadam* – prosperity; *vṛndāraṇya-kalinda-jā-jala-taṭe* – on the banks of the Yamunā in Vṛndāvana; *janma* – birth; *astu* – let there be; *lakṣāvadhi* – hundreds of thousands.

Translation

Who are all these learned scholars whose sophisticated minds are engaged in reflecting on various treatises, and who am I but a fool whose mind is fixed on the desire for Śyāma, Whose hue is like that of a new cloud? I do not long for family, wealth, power, respect or prosperity. I only wish to take hundreds of thousands of births on the banks of the Yamunā in Vṛndāvana.

TEXT 77

रम्यद्वीपसमुद्रपर्वतलसद्भूमण्डलाखण्डला-
खण्डैश्वर्यसुखानि यानि भुवने तिष्ठन्ति तान्येकतः ।
श्रीवृन्दावनकुञ्जपुञ्जविलसद्गोविन्दपादानुग-
प्रेमाश्लेषविशेषसौख्यसमता नास्त्येव नास्त्येव तैः ॥ ७७ ॥

ramya-dvīpa-samudra-parvata-lasad-bhū-maṇḍalākhaṇḍalā-
khaṇḍaiśvarya-sukhāni yāni bhuvane tiṣṭhanti tāny ekataḥ |
śrī-vṛndāvana-kuñja-puñja-vilasad-govinda-pādānuga-
premāśleṣa-viśeṣa-saukhya-samatā nāsty eva nāsty eva taiḥ || 77 ||

Word-For-Word Meanings

ramya- dvīpa- samudra- parvata- lasad- bhū-maṇḍalākhaṇḍalā-khaṇḍaiśvarya-sukhāni – the totality of all pleasures and opulences that exists in the three worlds, from the earth planet with its beautiful islands, oceans and mountains, up to Indra-loka; *yāni* – which; *bhuvane* – in the three worlds; *tiṣṭhanti* – exist; *tāni* – those; *ekataḥ* – all together; *śrī-vṛndāvana- kuñja- puñja- vilasad- govinda-pādānuga- premāśleṣa- viśeṣa-saukhya-samatā* – similarity with the particular happiness derived from lovingly embracing the lotus feet of Govinda, Who sports in the bowers of Śrī Vṛndāvana; *na* – not; *asti* – is; *eva* – indeed; *na* – not; *asti* – is; *eva* – indeed; *taiḥ* – with them.

Translation

The totality of all pleasures and opulences that exists in the three worlds, from the earth planet with its beautiful islands, oceans and mountains, up to Indra-loka, is nothing, really nothing like the particular happiness derived from lovingly embracing the lotus feet of Govinda, Who sports in the bowers of Śrī Vṛndāvana.

TEXT 78

रम्याखण्डलरत्नमण्डपलसच्छायासुखप्राप्तये
लोकौघः क्रकचव्यथामनुभवत्वेष प्रयागादिषु ।
जन्मान्तेषु पुनः पुनः पुनरहं श्रीराधिकावल्लभ-
प्रेमोल्लासलसत्कदम्बकुहरे जायेय कोऽप्यङ्घ्रिपः ॥ ७८ ॥

ramyākhaṇḍala-ratna-maṇḍapa-lasac-chāyā-sukha-prāptaye
lokaughaḥ krakaca-vyathām anubhavatv eṣa prayāgādiṣu |
janmānteṣu punaḥ punaḥ punar ahaṁ śrī-rādhikā-vallabha-
premollāsa-lasat-kadamba-kuhare jāyeya ko 'py aṅghripaḥ || 78 ||

Word-For-Word Meanings

ramyākhaṇḍala-ratna-maṇḍapa-lasac-chāyā-sukha-prāptaye – in order to attain pleasure from the glittering lights in the beautiful pavilions made of jewels in Indra-loka; *lokaughaḥ* – mob; *krakaca-vyathām* – hellish pain; *anubhavatu* – let them experience; *eṣaḥ* – this; *prayāgādiṣu* – in holy places such as Prayāga, etc.; *janmānteṣu* – in my next births; *punaḥ* – again; *punaḥ* – again; *punaḥ* – again; *aham* – I; *śrī-rādhikā-vallabha-premollāsa-lasat-kadamba-kuhare* – in the vicinity of those Kadamba trees that appear resplendent in joy out of love for the beloved of Śrīmatī Rādhikā; *jāyeya* – may I be born; *kaḥ api* – some; *aṅghripaḥ* – tree.

Translation

Let the mobs experience hellish pains while practising austerities in holy places such as Prayāga, etc., in order to attain pleasure from the glittering lights in the beautiful pavilions made of jewels in Indra-loka. In my next lives, I just wish to be born again and again and again as a tree in the vicinity of those Kadamba trees that appear resplendent in joy out of love for the beloved of Śrīmatī Rādhikā.

TEXT 79

कीटः कुञ्जकुटीतटीषु निवसन् भूपालकोटीरटन्
मत्तेभेन्द्रघटाविघट्टितरिपुप्रोद्यद्भुजाडम्बराः ।
स्वस्याधः कुरुते स्फुरत्कटिपटश्रीराधिकावल्लभ-
स्पृष्टाभीष्टलताविशिष्टविटपिप्राग्रं समाश्लिष्टवान् ॥ ७९ ॥

kīṭaḥ kuñja-kuṭī-taṭīṣu nivasan bhū-pāla-koṭīr aṭan
mattebhendra-ghaṭā-vighaṭṭita-ripu-prodyad-bhujāḍambarāḥ |
svasyādhaḥ kurute sphurat-kaṭi-paṭa-śrī-rādhikā-vallabha-
spṛṣṭābhīṣṭa-latā-viśiṣṭa-viṭapi-prāgraṁ samāśliṣṭavān || 79 ||

Word-For-Word Meanings

kīṭaḥ – an insect; *kuñja-kuṭī-taṭīṣu* – in the thresholds of cottages in the bowers; *nivasan* – living; *bhū-pāla-koṭīḥ* – millions of kings; *aṭan* – while roaming; *mattebhendra-ghaṭā-vighaṭṭita-ripu-prodyad-bhujāḍambarāḥ* – who proudly raise their arms after killing their enemies as if they were troops of mad kingly elephants; *svasya* – of oneself; *adhaḥ* – below; *kurute* – puts; *sphurat-kaṭi-paṭa-śrī-rādhikā-vallabha-spṛṣṭābhīṣṭa-latā-viśiṣṭa-viṭapi-prāgram* – the tip of a creeper or favourite tree touched by the beloved of Śrīmatī Rādhikā, who dresses in glittering skirts; *samāśliṣṭavān* – has embraced.

Translation

If while roaming about, an insect living in the thresholds of cottages in the bowers has embraced the tip of a creeper or favourite tree touched by the beloved of Śrīmatī Rādhikā, who dresses in glittering skirts, then it is far superior to millions of kings who proudly raise their arms after killing their enemies as if they were troops of mad kingly elephants.

TEXT 80

यत्रत्यैः शिखिभिः समानसकला ब्रह्मादयो निर्जरा
यत्पिच्छं मुकुटीकरोति शिरसि श्रीगोपचूडामणिः ।
तत्राहं वद नाथ केन विधिना जायेय वृन्दावने
सद्वृन्दा निवसन्ति यत्र दिविषद्वृन्दान्यधः कुर्वते ॥ ८० ॥

yatratyaiḥ śikhibhiḥ samāna-sakalā brahmādayo nirjarā
yat-piccham mukuṭī-karoti śirasi śrī-gopa-cūḍāmaṇiḥ |
tatrāham vada nātha kena vidhinā jāyeya vṛndāvane
sad-vṛndā nivasanti yatra diviṣad-vṛndāny adhaḥ kurvate || 80 ||

Word-For-Word Meanings

yatratyaiḥ – which dwell there; *śikhibhiḥ* – by the peacoks; *samāna-sakalāḥ* – on equal footing; *brahmādayaḥ* – Lord Brahmā, etc.; *nirjarāḥ* – demigods; *yat-piccham* – whose tail feather; *mukuṭī-karoti* – makes a crown; *śirasi* – on the head; *śrī-gopa-cūḍāmaṇiḥ* – the crest jewel of the cowherd men; *tatra* – there; *aham* – I; *vada* – tell; *nātha* – O Lord; *kena* – by which; *vidhinā* – method; *jāyeya* – may be born; *vṛndāvane* – in Vṛndāvana; *sad-vṛndāḥ* – groups of devotees; *nivasanti* – reside; *yatra* – where; *diviṣad-vṛndāni* - upon the hosts of heavenly denizens; *adhaḥ kurvate* – look down on.

Translation

Demigods like Lord Brahmā and others are on equal footing with the peacocks there, with whose tail feathers the crest jewel of the cowherd men makes a crown for His head. O Lord, please tell me by what method I can be born in that Vṛndāvana, where groups of devotees reside and look down even on the hosts of heavenly denizens.

TEXT 81

विभ्राणः करकं कणं च समदन्नेको वसेयं वने
किं कुर्वे करकङ्कणं क्षितिभुजां यत्सेवयासादितम् ।
तन्नामाङ्कितशंखचक्रधरणं पुण्यं हरेश्चन्दनं
तद्भक्ताभरणं तदेव किमु तैस्तुच्छैर्व्रजाधीश्वर ॥ ८१ ॥

vibhrāṇaḥ karakaṁ kaṇaṁ ca samadann eko vaseyaṁ vane
kiṁ kurve kara-kaṅkaṇaṁ kṣiti-bhujāṁ yat sevayāsāditam |
tan-nāmāṅkita-śaṅkha-cakra-dharaṇaṁ puṇyaṁ hareś candanaṁ
tad-bhaktābharaṇaṁ tad eva kim u tais tucchair vrajādhīśvara || 81 ||

Word-For-Word Meanings

vibhrāṇaḥ – holding; *karakam* – water pot; *kaṇam* – little; *ca* – and; *samadan* – eating; *ekaḥ* – alone; *vaseyam* – should live; *vane* – in the forest; *kim* – what; *kurve* – should do; *kara-kaṅkaṇam* – ornaments for the hand; *kṣiti-bhujām* – of kings; *yat* – which; *sevayā* – by serving; *āsāditam* – obtained; *tan-nāmāṅkita-śaṅkha-cakra-dharaṇam* – bearing conch, disc and marked with His Holy Names; *puṇyam* – pious; *hareḥ* – of Lord Hari; *candanam* – sandalwood paste; *tad-bhaktābharaṇam* – the ornament of His devotees; *tat* – that; *eva* – only; *kim u taiḥ* – what is the use of those; *tucchaiḥ* – insignificant; *vrajādhīśvara* – O Lord of Vraja.

Translation

What shall I do? Should I live alone in the forest holding a water pot and eating only a little? The pious sandalwood paste offered to Lord Hari, with which conch, disc and His Holy Names are marked,[8] is the only ornament of His devotees. O Lord of Vraja, what is the use of insignificant ornaments which were obtained by serving mundane kings?

8. Among South Indian Vaiṣṇavas it is common to mark the body with such symbols utilizing sandalwood paste.

TEXT 82

कदाहं त्वत्पादानुचरवरसेवास्वभिरतो
वसेयं श्रीवृन्दावनतटकुटीरद्रुमतले ।
दृशं ते कारुण्यामृतलहरिलावण्यललितां
व्रजाधीश स्वस्योपरि परम काङ्क्षामि सुखदाम् ॥ ८२ ॥

kadāhaṁ tvat-pādānucara-vara-sevā-svabhirato
vaseyaṁ śrī-vṛndāvana-taṭa-kuṭīra-druma-tale |
dṛśaṁ te kāruṇyāmṛta-lahari-lāvaṇya-lalitāṁ
vrajādhīśa svasyopari parama kāṅkṣāmi sukhadām || 82 ||

Word-For-Word Meanings

kadā – when; *aham* – I; *tvat-pādānucara-vara-sevā-svabhirataḥ* – thoroughly engaged in the service of the best servants of Your lotus feet; *vaseyam* – would live; *śrī-vṛndāvana-taṭa-kuṭīra-druma-tale* – under a tree or in a hut on the outskirts of Śrī Vṛndāvana; *dṛśam* – glance; *te* – Your; *kāruṇyāmṛta-lahari-lāvaṇya-lalitām* – charming and beautiful like waves of nectarean mercy; *vrajādhīśa* – O Lord of Vraja; *svasya* – of myself; *upari* – upon; *parama* – O Supreme; *kāṅkṣāmi* – eagerly desire; *sukhadām* – which gives great delight.

Translation

O Lord of Vraja, when shall I live under a tree or in a hut on the outskirts of Śrī Vṛndāvana and be thoroughly engaged in the service of the best servants of Your lotus feet? O Supreme, I eagerly desire to have upon me Your charming and beautiful glance, which is like waves of nectarean mercy and gives great delight.

TEXT 83

कदम्बतलनिर्मलक्षितिविलासकारी विभुः
सरोजदललोचनो नवपयोदनीलच्छविः ।
स्वकीयपदपङ्कजप्रणतिसार्थकं मे शिरो
विधातुमभि तद्वनं प्रतिसमाधयेन्मां कदा ॥ ८३ ॥

kadamba-tala-nirmala-kṣiti-vilāsa-kārī vibhuḥ
saroja-dala-locano nava-payoda-nīla-cchaviḥ |
svakīya-pada-paṅkaja-praṇati-sārthakaṁ me śiro
vidhātum abhi tad vanaṁ pratisamādhayen māṁ kadā || 83 ||

Word-For-Word Meanings

kadamba-tala-nirmala-kṣiti-vilāsa-kārī – Who performs amorous pastimes on the spotless soil under the Kadamba trees; *vibhuḥ* – the mighty Lord; *saroja-dala-locanaḥ* – Whose eyes are like lotus petals; *nava-payoda-nīla-cchaviḥ* – Whose hue is deep blue like a new cloud; *svakīya-pada-paṅkaja-praṇati-sārthakam* – meaningful by bowing down at His lotus feet; *me* – my; *śiraḥ* – head; *vidhātum* – make; *abhi* – towards; *tat* – that; *vanam* – forest; *pratisamādhayet* – direct; *mām* – me; *kadā* – when.

Translation

The mighty Lord Whose eyes are like lotus petals and Whose hue is deep blue like a new cloud performs amorous pastimes on the spotless soil under the shade of the Kadamba trees. When will He direct me towards that forest to make my head meaningful by bowing down at His lotus feet?

TEXT 84

कदाहं सन्द्रक्ष्ये तरणितनयातीरतरुणी-
कदम्बक्रीडायां निहितमनसं सुन्दरवरम् ।
भ्रमद्भ्रूचापश्रीकृतमदनकोदण्डदलनं
स्फुरद्दन्तज्योत्स्नादलितशिखराशेषकिरणम् ॥ ८४ ॥

kadāhaṁ sandrakṣye taraṇi-tanayā-tīra-taruṇī-
kadamba-krīḍāyāṁ nihita-manasaṁ sundara-varam |
bhramad-bhrū-cāpa-śrī-kṛta-madana-kodaṇḍa-dalanaṁ
sphurad-danta-jyotsnā-dalita-śikharāśeṣa-kiraṇam || 84 ||

Word-For-Word Meanings

kadā – when; *aham* – I; *sandrakṣye* – shall see; *taraṇi-tanayā-tīra-taruṇī-kadamba-krīḍāyām* – on playing with groups of damsels on the bank of the river Yamunā; *nihita-manasam* – Whose mind is fixed; *sundara- varam* – the most beautiful person; *bhramad-bhrū-cāpa-śrī-kṛta-madana-kodaṇḍa-dalanam* – Who breaks Cupid's bow with the beauty of the bows of His flickering eye-brows; *sphurad-danta-jyotsnā-dalita-śikharāśeṣa-kiraṇam* – Who defeats the sun rays reflected on the top of the mountains by the brightness of His shining teeth.

Translation

When shall I see the most beautiful person with His mind fixed on playing with groups of damsels on the bank of the river Yamunā? He breaks Cupid's bow with the beauty of the bows of His flickering eye-brows. The sun rays reflected on the top of the mountains are defeated by the brightness of His shining teeth.

TEXT 85

क्वाहं मन्दस्तव जनपदाम्भोजवैमुख्यकारी
क्व त्वं सेवासुलभचरणो भक्तलोकानुरक्तः ।
जाने जन्मावलिरनघ मे यास्यति स्वार्थशून्या
धन्यानां तन्नयनविषयं कृष्ण वृन्दावनं स्यात् ॥ ८५ ॥

kvāhaṁ mandas tava jana-padāmbhoja-vaimukhya-kārī
kva tvaṁ sevā-sulabha-caraṇo bhakta-lokānuraktaḥ |
jāne janmāvalir anagha me yāsyati svārtha-śūnyā
dhanyānāṁ tan nayana-viṣayaṁ kṛṣṇa vṛndāvanaṁ syāt || 85 ||

Word-For-Word Meanings

kva – where; *aham* – I; *mandaḥ* – dull-headed; *tava* – Your; *jana-padāmbhoja-vaimukhya-kārī* – averse to the lotus feet of Your devotees; *kva* – where; *tvam* – You; *sevā-sulabha-caraṇaḥ* – Whose feet are easily attainable by devotional service; *bhakta-lokānuraktaḥ* – attached to Your devotees; *jāne* – I know; *janmāvaliḥ* – series of births; *anagha* – O faultless one; *me* – my; *yāsyati* – will pass; *svārtha-śūnyā* – devoid of selfishness; *dhanyānām* – of the virtuous; *tat* – that; *nayana-viṣayam* – object to the eyes; *kṛṣṇa* – O Kṛṣṇa; *vṛndāvanam* – Vṛndāvana; *syāt* – would be.

Translation

Who am I, so dull-headed and averse to the lotus feet of Your devotees? And Who are You, so attached to Your devotees and Whose feet are easily attainable by devotional service? O faultless Kṛṣṇa, I know that I still need a series of births devoid of selfishness, for Vṛndāvana can be the object of vision only for those who are virtuous.

TEXT 86

अम्भःप्राप्त्यै जलदपटलं याचमानस्य नित्यं
कालो भूयान् विलयमगमच्चातकस्यात्मबन्धो ।
एवं यास्यत्यहह मथुरादर्शनाकाङ्क्षिणो मे
जाने जन्मावधिमयि हरे नैव मे नाथ दुःखम् ॥ ८६ ॥

ambhaḥ-prāptyai jalada-paṭalaṁ yācamānasya nityaṁ
kālo bhūyān vilayam agamac cātakasyātma-bandho |
evaṁ yāsyaty ahaha mathurā-darśanākāṅkṣiṇo me
jāne janmāvadhim ayi hare naiva me nātha duḥkham || 86 ||

Word-For-Word Meanings

ambhaḥ-prāptyai – to get water; *jalada-paṭalam* – a mass of clouds; *yācamānasya* – begging; *nityam* – constantly; *kālaḥ* – time; *bhūyān* – very much; *vilayam* – end; *agamat* – came; *cātakasya* – of the *cātaka* bird; *ātma-bandho* – O friend of the soul; *evam* – in this way; *yāsyati* – will pass; *ahaha* – alas; *mathurā-darśanākāṅkṣiṇaḥ* – desiring to see Mathurā; *me* – my; *jāne* – know; *janmāvadhim* – life span; *ayi hare* – O Lord Hari; *na* – not; *eva* – indeed; *me* – my; *nātha* – Lord; *duḥkham* – unfortunately.

Translation

O friend of the soul, the life span of the *cātaka* bird passes while constantly begging a mass of clouds for water.

Alas, will my time be spent like that while desiring to see Mathurā? O Lord Hari, unfortunately I do not know my life span.

TEXT 87

भोक्तुं पादपपादमूलपतितं पत्रं प्रशस्तं वने
श्रीवृन्दावननाम्नि नाथ सुखदं वृक्षत्वगाच्छादनम् ।
सर्पिःक्षीरसितासमेतमसकृन्नान्यत्र शाल्योदनं
नो पट्टाम्बरधारणं व्रजपते तत्सर्वमङ्गीकृतम् ॥ ८७ ॥

bhoktuṁ pādapa-pāda-mūla-patitaṁ patraṁ praśastaṁ vane
śrī-vṛndāvana-nāmni nātha sukhadaṁ vṛkṣa-tvag-ācchādanam |
sarpiḥ-kṣīra-sitā-sametam asakṛn nānyatra śālyodanaṁ
no paṭṭāmbara-dhāraṇaṁ vraja-pate tat sarvam aṅgīkṛtam || 87 ||

Word-For-Word Meanings

bhoktum – to enjoy; *pādapa-pāda-mūla-patitam* – fallen under the trees; *patram* – leaf; *praśastam* – best; *vane* – in the forest; *śrī-vṛndāvana- nāmni* – called Vṛndāvana; *nātha* – O Lord; *sukhadam* – pleasant; *vṛkṣa-tvag-ācchādanam* – covering with barks; *sarpiḥ-kṣīra-sitā-sametam* – with ghee, milk and sugar; *asakṛt* – repeatedly; *na* – not; *anyatra* – somewhere else; *śālyodanam* – cooked rice; *na u* – nor; *paṭṭāmbara-dhāraṇam* – wearing fine garments; *vraja-pate* – O Lord of Vraja; *tat* – that; *sarvam* – all; *aṅgīkṛtam* – agreed.

Translation

O Lord, it is best to take leaves fallen under the trees and cover oneself with pleasant barks in the forest called Śrī

Vṛndāvana, not repeatedly taking rice cooked with ghee, milk and sugar, nor wearing fine garments somewhere else. O Lord of Vraja, I have agreed to all these.

TEXT 88

सत्सङ्गे सति नाथ ते गुणकथापीयूषपानान्मम
क्षुत्तृण्मोहमदाधयो न हृदयं विध्यन्ति न व्याधयः ।
किन्त्वानन्दसमुद्रमज्जनवशाद्विश्वं च विस्मर्यते
त्वद्द्वारं सनकादिसेवितमतो लभ्येत तन्मे कथम् ॥ ८८ ॥

sat-saṅge sati nātha te guṇa-kathā-pīyūṣa-pānān mama
kṣut-tṛṇ-moha-madādhayo na hṛdayaṁ vidhyanti na vyādhayaḥ |
kintv ānanda-samudra-majjana-vaśād viśvaṁ ca vismaryate
tvad-dvāraṁ sanakādi-sevitam ato labhyeta tan me katham || 88 ||

Word-For-Word Meanings

sat-saṅge – in the association of saintly person; *sati* – there being; *nātha* – O Lord; *te* – Your; *guṇa-kathā-pīyūṣa-pānāt* – by drinking the nectar of the narration of Your transcendental qualities; *mama* – my; *kṣut-tṛṇ-moha-madādhayaḥ* – hunger, thirst, delusion, madness and anxiety; *na* – not; *hṛdayam* – heart; *vidhyanti* – pierce; *na* – nor; *vyādhayaḥ* – ailments; *kintu* – but; *ānanda-samudra-majjana-vaśāt* – by merging in the ocean of bliss; *viśvam* – the world; *ca* – and; *vismaryate* – is forgotten; *tvad-dvāram* – Your door; *sanakādi-sevitam* – worshipped by sages like the four Kumāras and others; *ataḥ* – therefore; *labhyeta* – may be attained; *tat* – that; *me* – to me; *katham* – how.

Translation

O Lord, by drinking the nectar of the narration of Your transcendental qualities in the association of saintly persons, hunger, thirst, delusion, madness, anxiety and ailments do not pierce my heart. Rather, by merging in the ocean of bliss, one forgets the whole world. Therefore, please tell me how I can attain Your door, which is resorted to by sages like the four Kumāras and others.

TEXT 89

कोऽपि स्यां तृणगुल्मपादपलतावल्लीषु वृन्दावने
भासश्येनकपोतकोकिलभरद्वाजाख्यबर्हिष्वपि ।
गोसिंहद्विपखड्गशल्लकशशन्यंकुद्विरेफादिषु
श्रीमद्गोकुलनाथ मानुषजनुर्नाहं पुनः प्रार्थये ॥ ८९ ॥

ko 'pi syāṁ tṛṇa-gulma-pādapa-latā-vallīṣu vṛndāvane
bhāsa-śyena-kapota-kokila-bharadvājākhya-barhiṣv api |
go-siṁha-dvipa-khaḍga-śallaka-śaśa-nyaṅku-dvirephādiṣu
śrīmad-gokula-nātha mānuṣa-janur nāhaṁ punaḥ prārthaye || 89 ||

Word-For-Word Meanings

kaḥ api – anyone; *syām* – let me be; *tṛṇa-gulma-pādapa-latā-vallīṣu* – among the creepers, trees, bushes or grass; *vṛndāvane* – in Vṛndāvana; *bhāsa-śyena-kapota-kokila-bharadvājākhya-barhiṣu* – among the peacocks, skylarks, cuckoos, doves, eagles or vultures; *api* – even; *go-siṁha-dvipa-khaḍga-śallaka-śaśa-nyaṅku-dvirephādiṣu* – among the cows, lions, elephants, rhinoceroses, porcupines, rabbits, antelopes or bumblebees; *śrīmad-gokula-nātha* – O glorious Lord of Gokula; *mānuṣa-januḥ* – human birth; *na* – not; *aham* – I; *punaḥ* – again; *prārthaye* – pray.

Translation

Let me be any living entity in Vṛndāvana among the creepers, trees, bushes or grass, among the peacocks, skylarks, cuckoos, doves, eagles or vultures, or even among the cows, lions, elephants, rhinoceroses, porcupines, rabbits, antelopes or bumblebees. O glorious Lord of Gokula, I do not pray for a human birth again.

TEXT 90

भाग्यं भूरि तदेव नाथ यमुनातीरस्थवृन्दावने
भूत्वा कोऽपि विलोकयेत्तव वपुर्नीलाम्बुदश्यामलम् ।
लब्ध्वा मानुषजन्म चेन्न भगवत्पादौ भजेत्सर्वदा
जातः किं न तदा तदीयजननीगर्भप्रपातः प्रभो ॥ ९० ॥

bhāgyaṁ bhūri tad eva nātha yamunā-tīra-stha-vṛndāvane
bhūtvā ko 'pi vilokayet tava vapur nīlāmbuda-śyāmalam |
labdhvā mānuṣa-janma cen na bhagavat-pādau bhajet sarvadā
jātaḥ kiṁ na tadā tadīya-jananī-garbha-prapātaḥ prabho || 90 ||

Word-For-Word Meanings

bhāgyam – good fortune; *bhūri* – very much; *tat* – that; *eva* – indeed; *nātha* – O Lord; *yamunā-tīra-stha-vṛndāvane* – in Vṛndāvana, which is situated on the banks of the Yamunā; *bhūtvā* – having been born; *kaḥ api* – someone; *vilokayet* – would behold; *tava* – Your; *vapuḥ* – beautiful form;

nīlāmbuda-śyāmalam – deep blue like a cloud; *labdhvā* – having obtained; *mānuṣa-janma* – human birth; *cet* – if; *na* – not; *bhagavat- pādau* – the lotus feet of the Supreme Lord; *bhajet* – would not worship; *sarvadā* – always; *jātaḥ* – born; *kiṁ na* – is it not; *tadā* – then; *tadīya-jananī-garbha-prapātaḥ* – an aborted offspring of his mother; *prabho* – O Master.

Translation

O Lord, it is very good fortune if one is born in Vṛndāvana, on the banks of the Yamunā, and thus beholds Your beautiful form, which is deep blue like a cloud. O Master, having obtained a human birth, if one does not always worship the lotus feet of the Supreme Lord, is he not like an aborted offspring of his mother?

TEXT 91

मत्तोऽन्यत्र सतः कलिन्दतनयातीरे पुलिन्दो वरं
योऽसौ पश्यति रासनर्तितवधूराजद्विहाराजिरम् ।
दृश्यन्तेऽविरतं मया धनमदप्रोत्फुल्लनासापुट-
स्तब्धभ्रूकुटिधारिणां विषयिणां द्वाराणि दुर्बुद्धिना ॥ ९१ ॥

matto 'nyatra sataḥ kalinda-tanayā-tīre pulindo varaṁ
yo 'sau paśyati rāsa-nartita-vadhū-rājad-vihārājiram |
dṛśyante 'viratam mayā dhana-mada-protphulla-nāsā-puṭa-
stabdha-bhrū-kuṭi-dhāriṇāṁ viṣayiṇāṁ dvārāṇi durbuddhinā || 91 ||

Word-For-Word Meanings

mattaḥ – than me; *anyatra* – elsewhere; *sataḥ* – being;

kalinda-tanayā- tīre – on the banks of the Yamunā; *pulindaḥ* – a savage; *varam* – better; *yaḥ* – who; *asau* – that; *paśyati* – beholds; *rāsa-nartita-vadhū-rājad-vihārājiram* – the shining arena of the *rāsa* dance of the damsels of Vraja; *dṛśyante* – is seen; *aviratam* – constantly; *mayā* – by me; *dhana-mada-protphulla-nāsā-puṭa-stabdha-bhrū-kuṭi-dhāriṇām* – with widely open nostrils and frowning eyebrows due to the intoxication of wealth; *viṣayiṇām* – of materialists; *dvārāṇi* – doors; *durbuddhinā* – foolish.

Translation

Even a savage who beholds the shining arena of the *rāsa* dance of the damsels of Vraja on the banks of the Yamunā is better than I, who am situated elsewhere. I am so foolish that all I see constantly is the doors of materialists with frowning eyebrows and raised noses due to the intoxication of wealth.

TEXT 92

न स्थानं न च मन्दिरं न मृदुलं तल्पं न पट्टाम्बरं
नो पुष्पाणि न चन्दनं सुरुचिरं नो शाकपाकक्रिया ।
कर्पूरं न शुभं न वा मृगमदो नो नागवल्लीदलं
किं ते नाथ समर्पयामि सुहृदे तेन व्यथा मे हृदि ॥ ९२ ॥

na sthānaṁ na ca mandiraṁ na mṛdulaṁ talpaṁ na paṭṭāmbaraṁ
no puṣpāṇi na candanaṁ suruciraṁ no śāka-pāka-kriyā |
karpūraṁ na śubhaṁ na vā mṛgamado no nāgavallī-dalaṁ
kiṁ te nātha samarpayāmi suhṛde tena vyathā me hṛdi || 92 ||

Word-For-Word Meanings

na – not; *sthānam* – a place; *na* – not; *ca* – and; *mandiram* – a temple; *na* – nor; *mṛdulam* – soft; *talpam* – a bed; *na* – nor; *paṭṭāmbaram* – fine garment; *na u* – nor; *puṣpāṇi* – flowers; *na* – nor; *candanam* – sandalwood; *suruciram* – pleasant; *na u* – nor; *śāka-pāka-kriyā* – cooked vegetables; *karpūram* – camphor; *na* – nor; *śubham* – good; *na* – not; *vā* – or; *mṛgamadaḥ* – musk; *na u* – nor; *nāgavallī-dalam* – betel leaf; *kim* – what; *te* – to You; *nātha* – O Lord; *samarpayāmi* – I offer; *suhṛde* – friend; *tena* – by this; *vyathā* – palpitation; *me* – my; *hṛdi* – in the heart.

Translation

If neither a place, a temple, a soft bed, nor fine garments, flowers, pleasant sandalwood or nice cooked vegetables, nor good camphor, musk or betel leaves, then what else should I offer to You, my friend? My heart palpitates because of this.

TEXT 93

अविरलगलदश्रुः प्रेमरुद्धस्खलद्गीर्
उपचितपुलकालीदेहलालित्यशाली ।
अविरतमभिजल्पन्नाम ते श्याम वृन्दा-
वनभुवि मुदितोऽहं तत् कदा पर्यटामि ॥ ९३ ॥

avirala-galad-aśruḥ prema-ruddha-skhalad-gīr
upacita-pulakālī-deha-lālitya-śālī |
aviratam abhijalpan nāma te śyāma vṛndā-
vana-bhuvi mudito 'haṁ tat kadā paryaṭāmi || 93 ||

Word-For-Word Meanings

avirala-galad-aśruḥ – incessantly shedding tears; *prema-ruddha-skhalad-gīḥ* – with a faltering voice, being overtaken by love; *upacita-pulakālī-deha-lālitya-śālī* – having a gracious form as one of Your girlfriends, having hairs standing on end; *aviratam* – constantly; *abhijalpan* – chanting; *nāma* – Holy Name; *te* – Your; *śyāma* – O Śyāma; *vṛndāvana-bhuvi* – in the land of Vṛndāvana; *muditaḥ* – glad; *aham* – I; *tat* – there; *kadā* – when; *paryaṭāmi* – roam.

Translation

O Śyāma, when shall I gladly roam in the land of Vṛndāvana constantly chanting Your Holy Name, incessantly shedding tears, overtaken by love, with a faltering voice, my hairs standing on end, having a gracious form as one of Your girlfriends?

TEXT 94

धरिष्यति न वा हरिस्त्रिदशचक्रचूडामणिर्
वचः श्रुतिपथे मम प्रकृतिदैन्यभाजो भुवि ।
इति प्रबलचिन्तया चपलमेव चेतोऽधुना
दधाति भयमुत्कटं व्रजकुलेन्द्र किं कुर्महे ॥ ९४ ॥

dhariṣyati na vā haris tri-daśa-cakra-cūḍāmaṇir
vacaḥ śruti-pathe mama prakṛti-dainya-bhājo bhuvi |
iti prabala-cintayā capalam eva ceto 'dhunā
dadhāti bhayam utkaṭaṁ vraja-kulendra kiṁ kurmahe || 94 ||

Word-For-Word Meanings

dhariṣyati – will place; *na* – not; *vā* – indeed; *hariḥ* – Lord Hari; *tri-daśa-cakra-cūḍāmaṇiḥ* – the crest jewel among the hosts of divinities; *vacaḥ* – instruction; *śruti-pathe* – in the auditory passage; *mama* – my; *prakṛti-dainya-bhājaḥ* – experiencing the distress caused by the material energy; *bhuvi* – in this world; *iti* – thus; *prabala-cintayā* – by thinking intensely; *capalam* – flickering; *eva* – indeed; *cetaḥ* – mind; *adhunā* – now; *dadhāti* – undergoes; *bhayam* – fear; *utkaṭam* – great; *vraja-kulendra* – O King of the inhabitants of Vraja; *kim* – what; *kurmahe* – we do.

Translation

Will Lord Hari, the crest jewel among all divinities, not place His instructions in my ears, suffering as I am in this world due to the material energy? Thinking intensely about this, my flickering mind now experiences great fear. O King of the inhabitants of Vraja, what should I do?

TEXT 95

ब्रह्मज्ञानकथा वृथा यदि हरेः सेवा न सम्पाद्यते
मिथ्या कर्मसु कौशलं यदि हरेरर्चा न सम्यक्कृता।
धर्मः शर्म करोति नैव हरये सम्यङ् न चेदर्पितो
याचेऽहं प्रतिजन्म नाथ भवतो दास्यं न हास्यं यतः ॥ ९५ ॥

brahma-jñāna-kathā vṛthā yadi hareḥ sevā na sampādyate
mithyā karmasu kauśalaṁ yadi harer arcā na samyak kṛtā |
dharmaḥ śarma karoti naiva haraye samyaṅ na ced arpito
yāce 'haṁ pratijanma nātha bhavato dāsyaṁ na hāsyaṁ yataḥ || 95 ||

Word-For-Word Meanings

brahma-jñāna-kathā – discussions about spiritual knowledge; *vṛthā* – useless; *yadi* – if; *hareḥ* – of Lord Hari; *sevā* – service; *na* – not; *sampādyate* – is brought about; *mithyā* – in vain; *karmasu* – in ritualistic activities; *kauśalam* – expertise; *yadi* – if; *hareḥ* – of Lord Hari; *arcā* – worship; *na* – not; *samyak* – properly; *kṛtā* – done; *dharmaḥ* – religious principles; *śarma* – happiness; *karoti* – produces; *na* – not; *eva* – indeed; *haraye* – to Lord Hari; *samyak* – duly; *na* – not; *cet* – if; *arpitaḥ* – offered; *yāce* – ask; *aham* – I; *pratijanma* – at every birth; *nātha* – O Lord; *bhavataḥ* – Your; *dāsyam* – servitude; *na* – not; *hāsyam* – derision; *yataḥ* – because of this.

Translation

Discussions about spiritual knowledge are useless if they do not bring about service to Lord Hari. Expertise in ritualistic activities is in vain if the worship of Lord Hari is not properly done. The observance of *dharma* produces no happiness if it is not duly offered to Lord Hari. O Lord, I only ask for the opportunity to serve You in every birth. Please do not deride my request.

TEXT 96

दुर्वारा जनता ददाति विविधक्लेशानियं दुःसहांस्
तस्यां सम्पतितो भवामि पतितो गोपाल मामुद्धर ।
मामाज्ञापय नाथ वस्तुमधुना वृन्दावने निर्जने
स्थित्वा कुञ्जकुटीतटे पटुरटन्नामैव नान्यद् ब्रुवे ॥ ९६ ॥

durvārā janatā dadāti vividha-kleśān iyaṁ duḥsahāṁs
tasyāṁ sampatito bhavāmi patito gopāla mām uddhara |
mām ājñāpaya nātha vastum adhunā vṛndāvane nirjane
sthitvā kuñja-kuṭī-taṭe paṭur aṭan nāmaiva nānyad bruve || 96 ||

Word-For-Word Meanings

durvārā – unrestrained; *janatā* – people; *dadāti* – give; *vividha-kleśān* – many kinds of sufferings; *iyam* – this; *duḥsahān* – unbearable; *tasyām* – among them; *sampatitaḥ* – fallen; *bhavāmi* – I am becoming; *patitaḥ* – degraded; *gopāla* – O Gopāla; *mām* – me; *uddhara* – save; *mām* – me; *ājñāpaya* – instruct; *nātha* – O Lord; *vastum* – the truth; *adhunā* – now; *vṛndāvane* – in Vṛndāvana; *nirjane* – in a solitary place; *sthitvā* – having been situated; *kuñja-kuṭī-taṭe* - on the threshold of a hut in the bowers; *paṭuḥ* – eloquent; *aṭan* – roaming about; *nāma* – Holy Name; *eva* – only; *na* – not; *anyat* – anything else; *bruve* – I speak.

Translation

These unrestrained people cause many kinds of sufferings which are unbearable. Having fallen among them, I am degrading myself. O Gopāla, please save me. O Lord, now please instruct me about the truth. Once situated on the threshold of a hut in the bowers in a solitary place in Vṛndāvana, I will roam about eloquently speaking only Your Holy Name and nothing else.

TEXT 97

दासास्ते जगतां त्रिकालसुखदास्तैः सङ्कुलः सङ्कुलो
न स्याद्वास इति प्रभो त्वदनुगैः साकं वसेयं वने ।

श्रीमत्तन्मुखपङ्कजच्युतकथापीयूषमत्यादृतो
नित्यं कर्णपुटैः पिबन् व्रजपते तिष्ठामि माद्यन्मनाः ॥ ९७ ॥

dāsās te jagatāṁ tri-kāla-sukhadās taiḥ saṅkulaḥ saṅkulo
na syād vāsa iti prabho tvad-anugaiḥ sākaṁ vaseyaṁ vane |
śrīmat-tan-mukha-paṅkaja-cyuta-kathā-pīyūṣam atyādṛto
nityaṁ karṇa-puṭaiḥ piban vraja-pate tiṣṭhāmi mādyan-manāḥ || 97 ||

Word-For-Word Meanings

dāsāḥ – servants; *te* – Your; *jagatām* – to the universe; *tri-kāla- sukhadāḥ* – giving happiness in the past, present and future; *taiḥ* – with them; *saṅkulaḥ* – full; *saṅkulaḥ* – distress; *na* – not; *syāt* – there would be; *vāse* – in a dwelling place; *iti* – thus; *prabho* – O Lord; *tvad-anugaiḥ* – with Your devotees; *sākam* – together; *vaseyam* – may I live; *vane* – in the forest; *śrīmat-tan-mukha-paṅkaja-cyuta-kathā-pīyūṣam* – the nectarean narrations streaming forth from their glorious lotus mouths; *atyādṛtaḥ* – very attentively; *nityam* – always; *karṇa-puṭaiḥ* – through the ears; *piban* – drinking; *vraja-pate* – O Lord of Vraja; *tiṣṭhāmi* – I remain; *mādyan-manāḥ* – whose heart is delighted.

Translation

Your servants always give great happiness to the whole universe, in the past, present and future, thus there should not be distress in a place full of them. Therefore, O Lord, please let me live in the forest accompanied by Your devotees. O Lord of Vraja, while very attentively drinking the nectarean narrations streaming forth from their glorious lotus mouths through my ears, I always remain very delighted at heart.

TEXT 98

तापाः कुत्र कथामृतानि पिबतः क्वासौ पुनः संसृतिः
शोकः कुत्र मदः क्व कुत्र विषयाः क्रोधः क्व कामः क्व वा ।
लोभः कुत्र तमः क्व कुत्र मरणाद्भीतिः क्व वा मत्सरः
कः सेवेत न ते स्फुरद्गुणकथां सत्कथ्यमानां बुधः ॥ ९८ ॥

tāpāḥ kutra kathāmṛtāni pibataḥ kvāsau punaḥ saṁsṛtiḥ
śokaḥ kutra madaḥ kva kutra viṣayāḥ krodhaḥ kva kāmaḥ kva vā |
lobhaḥ kutra tamaḥ kva kutra maraṇād bhītiḥ kva vā matsaraḥ
kaḥ seveta na te sphurad-guṇa-kathāṁ sat-kathyamānāṁ budhaḥ ||98||

Word-For-Word Meanings

tāpāḥ – the threefold miseries; *kutra* – where; *kathāmṛtāni* – nectarean topics; *pibataḥ* – for one drinking; *kva* – where; *asau* – that; *punaḥ* – again; *saṁsṛtiḥ* – the cycle of birth and death; *śokaḥ*- distress; *kutra* – where; *madaḥ* – madness; *kva* – where; *kutra* – where; *viṣayāḥ* – sensual enjoyment; *krodhaḥ* – anger; *kva* – where; *kāmaḥ* – lust; *kva* – where; *vā* – or; *lobhaḥ* – greed; *kutra* – where; *tamaḥ* – ignorance; *kva* – where; *kutra* – where; *maraṇāt* – of death; *bhītiḥ* – fear; *kva* – where; *vā* – or; *matsaraḥ* – envy; *kaḥ* – who; *seveta* – would honour; *na* – not; *te* – Your; *sphurad-guṇa-kathām* – the vibrant narrations about Your qualities; *sat-kathyamānām* – being spoken by the saintly devotees; *budhaḥ* – an intelligent person.

Translation

For one who is hearing the nectarean topics about You, where are the threefold miseries? Where is the cycle of birth and death? Where is distress, madness, sensual enjoyment, anger or lust? Where is greed, ignorance, envy or fear of death? Which intelligent person would not honour the vibrant narrations about Your qualities from the mouth of saintly devotees?

TEXT 99

श्रीमत्कृष्णकथा त्रितापशमनी शोकाब्धिसंशोषिणी
क्रोधध्वान्तविनाशिनी मदगजप्रोत्साहविध्वंसिनी ।
लोभारम्भविघट्टिनी विषयकृद्वैषम्यनिर्हारिणी
चित्तानन्दविवर्धिनी निजजनानेकप्रभाकारिणी ॥ ९९ ॥

śrīmat-kṛṣṇa-kathā tri-tāpa-śamanī śokābdhi-saṁśoṣiṇī
krodha-dhvānta-vināśinī mada-gaja-protsāha-vidhvaṁsinī |
lobhārambha-vighaṭṭinī viṣaya-kṛd-vaiṣamya-nirhāriṇī
cittānanda-vivardhinī nija-janān eka-prabhā-kāriṇī || 99 ||

Word-For-Word Meanings

śrīmat-kṛṣṇa-kathā – the glorious narrations about Lord Kṛṣṇa; *tri-tāpa-śamanī* – extinguishing the threefold miseries; *śokābdhi-saṁśoṣiṇī* – drying up the ocean of distress; *krodha-dhvānta-vināśinī* – annihilating the darkness of anger; *mada-gaja-protsāha-vidhvaṁsinī* – destroying the strength of the elephant of madness; *lobhārambha-vighaṭṭinī* – striking the actions of greed; *viṣaya-kṛd-vaiṣamya-nirhāriṇī* – removing the troubles caused by worldly life; *cittānanda-vivardhinī* – increasing the happiness in the heart; *nija-janān* – to His devotees; *eka-prabhā-kāriṇī* – the sole source of enlightenment.

Translation

The glorious narrations about Lord Kṛṣṇa extinguish the threefold miseries, dry up the ocean of distress, annihilate the darkness of anger, destroy the strength of the elephant of madness, strike the actions of greed, remove the troubles caused by worldly life, increase happiness in the heart, and are the sole source of enlightenment for His devotees.

TEXT 100

श्रीमत्कुण्डलमण्डिताननविधौ दन्तप्रभाकौमुदी-
विध्वस्तव्रजवल्लभाधितमसि प्रोत्फुल्लवक्त्राम्बुजे ।
वंशीनादविमोहिताखिलजगज्जन्तौ किशोराकृतौ
श्रीकृष्णे रतिरस्तु मे प्रतिघटि प्रेमाब्धिसंवर्धिनी ॥ १०० ॥

śrīmat-kuṇḍala-maṇḍitānana-vidhau danta-prabhā-kaumudī-
vidhvasta-vraja-vallabhādhi-tamasi protphulla-vaktrāmbuje |
vaṁśī-nāda-vimohitākhila-jagaj-jantau kiśorākṛtau
śrī-kṛṣṇe ratir astu me pratighaṭi premābdhi-saṁvardhinī || 100 ||

Word-For-Word Meanings

śrīmat-kuṇḍala-maṇḍitānana-vidhau – Whose moon-like face is decorated with gracious earrings; *danta-prabhā-kaumudī-vidhvasta-vraja-vallabhādhi-tamasi* – Who dissipates the darkness of the anxiety of the damsels of Vraja by the shining rays of His teeth; *protphulla-vaktrāmbuje* – Whose mouth is like a fully blossomed lotus; *vaṁśī-nāda-vimohitākhila-jagaj-jantau* – Whose flute sound bewilders all living entities in the universe; *kiśorākṛtau* – Whose form is youthful; *śrī- kṛṣṇe* – for Lord Kṛṣṇa; *ratiḥ* – devotion; *astu* – let there be; *me* – my; *pratighaṭi* – at every moment; *premābdhi-saṁvardhinī* – which increases the ocean of love.

Translation

At every moment, may I have such devotion which increases the ocean of love for Śrī Kṛṣṇa, Whose form is youthful, Whose flute sound bewilders all living entities in the universe, Whose moon-like face is decorated with gracious earrings, Whose mouth is like a fully blossomed lotus, and Who dissipates the darkness of the anxiety of the damsels of Vraja by the shining rays of His teeth.

iti śrī-prabodhānanda-sarasvatī-viracitaṁ viveka-śatakaṁ samāptam ||

Thus ends the *Viveka-śatakam* composed by Śrīla Prabodhānanda Sarasvatī.

|| śrī-śrī-rādhā-ramaṇa-tadīyārpaṇam astu ||

BALADEVA VIDYĀBHŪṢAṆA PROJECT

This publication is part of the Baladeva Vidyābhūṣaṇa Project, whose main objectives are as follows:

1. Search for lost manuscripts.
2. Digitally preserve manuscripts currently existing in different libraries.
3. Digitally preserve all editions of Vidyābhūṣaṇa's books.
4. Digitally preserve articles written about Vidyābhūṣaṇa.
5. Type the texts in digital unicode, which can be converted into Devanāgarī, Bengali characters, etc.
6. Prepare a critical edition of each work.
7. Translate all the works into English.
8. Publish all translations with the original Devanāgarī text.
9. Investigate and verify existent biographical data on Vidyābhūṣaṇa.
10. Publish a comprehensive biographical work.

For more details and for updated versions of the Sanskrit text, the readers are advised to visit the following page:

www.vidyabhusanaproject.blogspot.com

Bhakti Vikas Trust

Books by Bhakti Vikāsa Swami

A Beginner's Guide to Kṛṣṇa Consciousness

Read this book and improve your life!

All you need to know to get started in Kṛṣṇa consciousness. Easy-to-understand guidance on daily practices that bring us closer to Kṛṣṇa. Packed with practical information. Suitable both for devotees living in an ashram or at home.

A Message to the Youth of India

Youth of India, Awake!

Your country is destined to lead the world by spiritual strength. Understand the power of your own culture, which is attracting millions from all over the world.

Arise, come forward, be enlightened

Brahmacarya in Kṛṣṇa Consciousness

A "user's guide" to *brahmacārī* life. The first part consists of elaborate discussions and practical guidance regarding many aspects of *brahmacarya.* The second portion is a compilation of quotations on *brahmacarya* from Śrīla Prabhupāda's books, letters, and recordings.

Glimpses of Traditional Indian Life

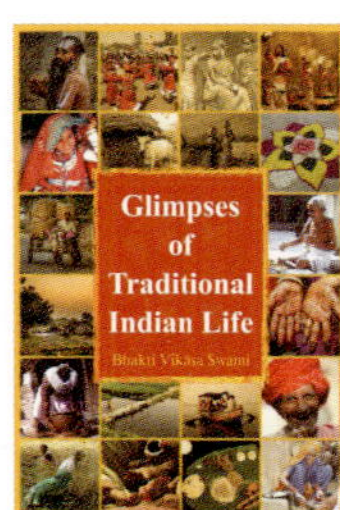

Journey to the real India. Discover the wisdom and devotion at the heart of Indian life. Meet people who were raised in a godly atmosphere and learn how it shaped their character and enriched their life. Explore the adverse effects of India's technological development, the downfall of her hereditary culture, and other causes of India's present degradation.

Jaya Śrīla Prabhupāda!

There is no limit to Śrīla Prabhupāda's transcendental attributes, nor do we wish to ever stop describing them. His qualities, combined with his achievements, undoubtedly establish Śrīla Prabhupāda as an extraordinarily great transcendental personality.

My Memories of Śrīla Prabhupāda

An ISKCON *sannyāsī* recalls his few but precious memories of the most significant personality to have graced the earth in recent times.

Also includes:

- On Serving Śrīla Prabhupāda in Separation
- Vyasa-pūjā Offerings

On Pilgrimage in Holy India

Travel with an ISKCON *sannyāsī*, including to some of India's less-known but most charming holy places.

On Speaking Strongly in Śrīla Prabhupāda's Service

Why followers of Śrīla Prabhupāda should speak strongly, as he did. A comprehensive analysis of how to present Kṛṣṇa consciousness straightforwardly, intelligently, and effectively. Features many anecdotes and more than five hundred powerful quotes.

Śrī Bhaktisiddhānta Vaibhava

Śrīla Bhaktisiddhānta Sarasvatī Ṭhākura altered the course of religious history by reviving and forcefully propagating pure Kṛṣṇa consciousness. His boldness in combating cheating religion earned him the appellation "lion guru"—yet his heart was soft with divine love for Kṛṣṇa.

Śrī Bhaktisiddhānta Vaibhava is presented in three volumes

Śrī Caitanya Mahāprabhu

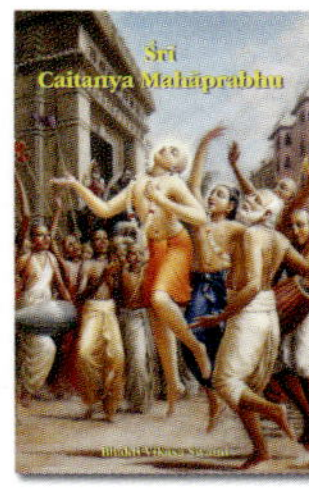

Hundreds of thousands of people throughout the world now follow the spotless path of Kṛṣṇa consciousness as given by Lord Caitanya. This book gives an overview of the life and teachings of Śrī Caitanya Mahāprabhu, the most munificent *avatāra* ever to grace this planet.

Śrī Vaṁśīdāsa Bābājī

Śrīla Vaṁsīdāsa Bābājī was a great Vaiṣṇava who although physically present in this world, had little communication with it. This book introduces us to a personality of such extraordinary, inscrutable character that we simply offer him obeisance and beg for his mercy.

The Story of Rasikānanda

Śrī Rasikānanda Deva was a mighty Vaiṣṇava *ācārya* in the era after Lord Caitanya's disappearance. Along with his guru, Śrīla Śyāmānanda Paṇḍita, he inundated North Orissa and surrounding districts in waves of Kṛṣṇa-*prema* that are still flowing today. The exciting story of Śrī Rasikānanda Deva is told herein.

Mothers and Masters

Mothers and Masters presents traditionalist arguments for the direction of the Kṛṣṇa consciousness movement, proposing that we should take up Śrīla Prabhupāda's mandate to establish *varṇāśrama-dharma* rather than capitulate to the norms and ideologies of secular culture.

Books by Other Authors

Śrī Cāṇakya-nīti (by Patita Pāvana Dāsa)

Practically every recorded statement that His Divine Grace Śrīla Prabhupāda ever made about the great Cāṇakya can be found here in this definitive edition. For the modern reader, the wisdom of Cāṇakya is nothing less than the key to a life that is in every way successful, happy and fulfilled.

Rethinking Darwin (by Lalitānātha Dāsa)

In Rethinking Darwin, Danish science writer Leif A. Jensen, in collaboration with leading Intelligent Design proponents such as Dr. Michael Behe, Dr. William Dembski, and Dr. Jonathan Wells, points out flaws in the Darwinian paradigm and examines the case for intelligent design.

Who is Supreme? (by Gokula Candra Dāsa)

Who, if any, among the plethora of gods and goddesses in the 'Hindu pantheon' is supreme? *Who Is Supreme?* tackles this riddle—not with the pablum and word jugglery characteristic of many of today's popular gurus, but with a straightforward and lucid analysis of the seminal sources of Vedic knowledge.